THE LIZARD KING

THE
LIZARD
KING

The True Crimes and Passions

of the World's Greatest

Reptile Smugglers

BRYAN CHRISTY

NEW YORK BOSTON

TWELVE

Twelve

Hachette Book Group USA

237 Park Avenue

New York, NY 10017

Visit our Web site at www.HachetteBookGroupUSA.com.

Twelve is an imprint of Grand Central Publishing.
The Twelve name and logo are trademarks of Hachette Book Group USA, Inc.

Book design by Fearn Cutler de Vicq

Printed in the United States of America

First Edition: August 2008

10 9 8 7 6 5 4 3 2 1

Library of Congress Cataloging-in-Publication Data

Christy, Bryan.
The lizard king : the true crimes and passions of the world's greatest
reptile smugglers / Bryan Christy.—1st ed.
p. cm.
ISBN-13: 978-0-446-58095-3
ISBN-10: 0-446-58095-3
1. Van Nostrand, Michael.   2. Van Nostrand, Raymond.
3. Reptile trade—United States.   4. Wildlife smuggling—
United States.   5. Animal dealers—United States.   I. Title.
SK593.R47C4 2008
364.1'8—dc22
2007049534

For my mother and father

They are not brethren, they are not underlings; they are other nations caught with ourselves in the net of life and time, fellow prisoners of the splendour and travail of the earth.

—Henry Beston, *The Outermost House:*
A Year of Life on the Great Beach of Cape Cod

Contents

THE LIZARD KING

The Argentine Conspiracy

He packed the baby tortoises like dia-monds, one to a pocket, and stapled each pocket closed. When he had ten pockets filled, he lifted the completed length of cloth and laid it with the others inside a hard-sided suit-case whose walls he had lined with thick foam. It was to be his last trip of the season, and he wanted to make the most of it. He repeated the process until all of the tortoises were packed. The snakes he tied inside pillowcases, and when he was done, he stuffed his laundry into the suitcase, including a little pink hairbrush he was bringing home to Miami as a gift.

Time is money. If you counted the time, which is to say if you calculated the odds that an overworked customs inspector would catch you and multiplied it by the prison time you would do if you were caught, reptiles were a good bet. First, nobody got caught; and then

even if you did, the penalty was not jail, it was a parking ticket. *Snakes?* Find a jury of twelve men and women
in any state in the union that would sentence a man to
prison for smuggling snakes. It was not going to happen.
You didn't go to prison for what he carried in his suitcase;
you killed it with a shovel.

He had tried birds, but birds died. Reptiles were
as durable and easy to pack as precious stones, without
the up-front costs. And the profit margins were as good
as cocaine without the machine guns or the felony drug
charges. Best of all, you weren't going up against the DEA
or the FBI, you were going up against the U.S. Fish and
Wildlife Service. Really, you would be stupid not to do it.

Not that he considered all of this himself. He was smart,
sure, but this was not his country. He was an Argentine
citizen with an American green card. The one who thought
about all of this and no doubt a lot more owned a company
called Strictly Reptiles, the largest reptile import-export
company in the United States. He did not interact with the
owner directly, but every decent reptile smuggler in the
country knew the name Mike Van Nostrand.

Tomas Medina, a computer-parts salesman, stepped
out of American Airlines Flight 900 on March 25, 1992,
wearing a gray business suit and a black necktie and passed
through U.S. immigration. It had been his twenty-seventh
birthday when he'd boarded the plane in Buenos Aires,
but now as he waited for his suitcase to arrive, it was a new
day and barely half past five on an overcast morning.

He heaved his suitcase off the conveyer and began
wheeling it toward customs. Traveling regularly between
Buenos Aires and Miami, Medina had become little more
than a computer part himself, delivering and receiving

instructions along a set pathway. Everyone at American Airlines knew his face, and so did many customs officers.

One of them was waving to him. It took a moment for the errant impulse to reach his brain, a moment more for his brain to process the information. Behind his eyeglasses, Medina blinked. The official was not waving. He was pointing, ordering him toward a line marked PLANT PROTECTION AND QUARANTINE.

There was nothing he could do. He obeyed. He lifted his suitcase onto an X-ray machine's conveyer belt and watched his future disappear.

Department of Agriculture inspector Lee Cross was a burly man who'd seen a good deal of smuggling and heard a good number of excuses. He studied the image on his X-ray screen; what he saw were two rows of unfamiliar dark objects. He asked Medina what they were. Medina joined Cross in looking at the X-ray screen. He saw what appeared to be two rows of black ravioli. "Turtles," he said.

The inspector looked again at the X-ray image, rubbing his beard. "Ceramic turtles?" he asked.

Medina said they were not ceramic.

Cross assumed Medina was bringing in Argentine handicrafts that were either undeclared or undervalued on his customs declaration form. It was hard to tell from the X-ray, but the way the items were layered, it looked like there might be quite a few of them.

"Wooden turtles?" he asked.

Again Medina said no.

"Well, sir," Cross asked, "what sort of turtles are we talking about?"

~~~~~

In 1981, Bob Clark, a frustrated clothing-store manager in Oklahoma City, thumbed his barbershop's *National Geographic* while he waited for a haircut. Married, earning just $14,000 a year, an underutilized master's degree in herpetology hanging limp around his neck, Clark began reading an exposé on international wildlife crime entitled "Wild Cargo: The Business of Smuggling Animals." The investigative report told the story of poachers after black rhinoceroses for their horns in Kenya, elephant ivory carvers in Hong Kong, Indian tiger hunters, and more. It also depicted the luxury end of the wildlife trade, much of it legal, including bear-paw soup in Macao, amber Japanese wedding combs made of sea turtles' shells, and lizard-skin boots for sale at Saks Fifth Avenue in New York.

When Clark turned the page, he gasped. A full-page photograph showed a pudgy Thai man dressed in a stylish brown shirt; he was holding a cordless telephone and grinning. The man's name was Mr. Dang. Around Mr. Dang's neck was looped a young Burmese python, one of the most common snake species in the U.S. pet trade. Dang was smiling because instead of the brown-and-copper coloring that marks a normal Burmese python, Dang's snake was pale yellow and white—an albino.

Clark began to tremble.

According to a caption beside the photograph, "Wildlife tycoon 'Mr. Dang' of Bangkok annually sells nearly a million dollars' worth of pets from Asia. This rare albino python could bring $20,000 in Germany, Japan, or the United States, his major outlets."

Clark was not sure Dang's figure was correct, but if it was even close Dang had grossly underestimated the potential of his reptile. Because Bob Clark, like relatively few others in the world at that time, knew how to make that python *breed*.

Clark was sandy-haired, fit, and as midwestern as corn. He'd gotten his master's at the University of Kansas; if there were an Ivy League for studying reptiles, the University of Kansas would have the rank of Harvard or Yale. His first thought at seeing the photograph was plain as milk: "I want *that* more than anything." In the weeks to come, it was all he thought about, all he talked about. He had the soft, joyous voice of a man touched by God. He drove his wife crazy going on about that photograph, but eventually he located the snake. It was no longer in Thailand. It was on the price list of a Florida reptile dealer named Tom Crutchfield, who had also read the *National Geographic* article.

By the time Crutchfield had figured out where the snake was, it and two others had been stolen from Dang and shipped to New York. The Thai government would be alerted and would attempt to retrieve the pythons without success. Ignorant of these details, Crutchfield remortgaged his house and bought all three snakes from a New York reptile dealer for $21,000. Then he boarded an airplane to go meet Dang in person. Dang dealt in albinos of many species, including wallabies, macaques, turtles, and cobras. Crutchfield's objective was to lock up the global market in albino Burmese pythons, and he did.

Crutchfield and Clark partnered to breed one of the albino pythons. In the summer of 1986 Bob Clark produced the world's first captive-bred clutch of albino Burmese pythons. To his delight, the babies were much brighter than Dang's wild-caught adult. They were a dazzling orange, gold, and white. At the time, normal Burmese pythons were wholesaling around the country for $30 each. With no idea what the market would bear, Clark priced his babies at $4,000 apiece. He only had six to sell, but he sold them all, virtually the day they were born. In his first try, Clark had nearly doubled his annual clothing-store salary. His second year, Bob Clark produced seventy albino babies. He sold those for $2,500 each. Demand increased. All over the United States men began borrowing money and remortgaging their homes, to go see Bob Clark.

Bob Clark was out of the clothing business, but there was still a problem. Burmese pythons are among the largest snakes in the world. Out of the egg, a Burmese python can grow to ten feet its first year. A fully grown adult can weigh over 250 pounds, wrap around a small car, and swallow a pig. The fact that normal versions of the snake sold so well in American pet shops was a tribute to the gullibility of parents everywhere and the boundless optimism of youth. The market for $2,500 monsters was more limited.

If nothing else had happened, Bob Clark's contribution would probably have given the reptile industry a bit of a bump before it then settled back down to its usual place at the bottom of the pet-shop barrel. Reptiles were traditionally the Bic lighters of the pet industry: cheap, disposable point-of-sale pets that were often a quick alternative to placate the child screaming for the $500 puppy in the window, a no-brainer gift for an uncle late to his niece's birthday party.

Clark had tapped into something unique. It wasn't albinism. There were already plenty of albino snakes among domestic U.S. species—kingsnakes and corn snakes, for example. It was the power to take a dream and change its color, to make it rare again. Reptile people are on a trajectory from the time they are children: *bigger, meaner, rarer, hot.* The boy who finds a garter snake and likes it soon wants something larger, often an imported python or boa constrictor. Not long after that he may want a meaner form of an animal—a kid who likes turtles might want a snapping turtle, for example. A desire for rarer animals reflects the hobbyist's deepening interest and the addictive quality of any hard-earned knowledge. *Hot* is slang for *venomous.* It can also, of course, refer to illegal. Most reptile enthusiasts give up their hobby long before the hot phase, and some never feel it at all. Still, few who get into the reptile world as children do not long, at some point, for something exotic, something imported.

About the size of a baseball bat, an African ball python is among the most popular imported snakes in America. In 1989, Bob Clark received a photograph in the mail of a young albino ball python recently caught in Ghana. He imported it, and in 1992 he produced the world's first clutch of captive-bred albino ball pythons. At the time, normal ball pythons (named for their tendency to roll into a ball when frightened) were selling for the same price they sell for today, roughly 30 bucks. Clark sold his albinos for $7,500 each. Out of nowhere, a Maryland man produced an albino boa constrictor and priced his offspring at $10,000 apiece. At forty babies in a boa constrictor clutch, that was $400,000 a year from just one snake.

Rumors of easy snake money flashed through the reptile world. Advertisements for "Investment Grade Reptiles!" were no joke. People began withdrawing savings, borrowing from family, selling off recreational vehicles to get in on snake money. In a reptilian version of *Jack and the Beanstalk*, a young Detroit man borrowed from his mother, flew to Oklahoma City, and bought $50,000 worth of Clark's albino Burmese pythons, just ten pairs. Instead of selling the resulting offspring, he rented a warehouse and hoarded them; four years later with five thousand Burmese pythons, Mark S. Bell and his wife bought a $1.2 million Florida property and launched a new era of reptile breeding: mass production.

Set up like a military base with temperature-controlled buildings, antibacterial shoe washes, and a high-security system, the Bells would soon receive deliveries that made their neighbors wonder: one million mealworms, fifty thousand crickets, and ten thousand frozen rodents—every week. The Bells' Reptile Industries would quadruple again, becoming the likely source today for the only reptiles many Americans will ever see: the baby snakes, lizards, and tortoises on sale in the country's largest pet-store chains.

Bob Clark would make millions as a snake breeder. He would appear on *Late Show with David Letterman*. Reptile breeders, hungry for their own gold mines, would soon begin "genetically designing" fantastic new colors and patterns, selling their creations for prices that would make Clark's albino Burmese python discovery seem "quaint"—$85,000 and more for a single snake.

Meantime, economic ripples continued to flow outward from Oklahoma City. The frozen-rodent delivery market blossomed. Owners of companies with names like Gourmet Rodent and Mice-on-Ice—selling pinkies, fuzzies, weanlings, rat pups, and jumbos packed in dry ice—saw their businesses climb, as did cricket ranchers and drosophila growers. Overnight shipping of reptiles and their food became second nature. Heating products, vitamin supplements, bedding, misting systems, and cage building expanded.

All of this new money was blood in the water to smugglers. Breeding reptiles and catching reptiles often appeal to two different personality types. Breeding reptiles takes the time, capital, and the patience of a farmer. Catching reptiles takes a pair of old boots and a plane ticket. There is a joke among reptile smugglers: what's the first thing that happens when a new reptile or amphibian species is discovered? Answer: two Germans buy plane tickets. All over the world nature produces plenty of rare species and she makes a lot more of them than any snake breeder can. Reptile smugglers, emboldened by snake money, fanned out across the globe, bringing in protected tortoises, turtles, frogs, salamanders, lizards, and snakes.

A single photograph had given birth to a new era, both legal and illegal. One company intended to profit from both sides of the law on a scale never before witnessed. It was called Strictly Reptiles, and it bought reptiles from breeders, exporters, and smugglers. Its impact on the reptile world would be enormous. When Mikhail Gorbachev opened Russia to trade, when Michael Jackson wanted a giant tortoise for his Neverland ranch, when the elite New York Explorers Club wanted to serve honey-glazed tarantula at its annual Waldorf-Astoria black-tie dinner— Strictly Reptiles would get the call. In a good year, any green iguana in any pet shop in America had a one-in-two chance of coming from Strictly Reptiles. It was in the top handful of the world's largest reptile import-export companies and its owner had visions of more.

And so when Tomas Medina stepped off that airplane with a suitcase full of Argentine reptiles, he did so not only as a reptile smuggler but also as a cog in a reptile industry quivering with new wealth.

New Agent in Town

The Miami office liked to spoil the new agents right off with an easy first case, and that's exactly what Special Agent Jennifer English of the U.S. Fish and Wildlife Service considered Tomas Medina on the morning of March 25, 1992. She got off the phone with airport customs and telephoned Chip Bepler at home, telling him they had stopped a mule bringing in turtles at Miami International. It would be his first time to see the airport since his transfer down from New York. Questioning a turtle smuggler was the perfect way to get Bepler's feet wet.

English pulled up to Bepler's home in her government car, a shabby cream-colored Crown Victoria LTD whose windows she had tinted herself using petty cash.

She'd helped Chip and his wife pick out their new house. It was a ranch-style home only a few miles from her own, a half hour north of Miami where, in her case, there was still a little green for her horses. The Beplers' was a nice little suburban neighborhood, halfway between the nearby Everglades and the Atlantic Ocean, where the lawn could be mowed in a beer or two and the children Chip and Robin were thinking about having would find plenty of friends to play with. There was a pond just up the road and Brian Piccolo Park was nearby, named for the football star who had died so unexpectedly of cancer.

Chip and Robin both worked for Fish and Wildlife. Robin was a wildlife inspector; Chip was a special agent. The couple had transferred to the Miami office as a double hire, based in part on English's recommendation. Like them, English had put in time in New York prior to her move to Florida, and for a while she and Robin had been wildlife inspectors together at JFK International Airport. Also like Robin, English had a husband who was a special agent.

To tell the truth, the Miami office probably needed Robin more than they needed Chip. At the major port cities—Los Angeles, Miami, and New York—more wildlife crime came and left packed in wooden crates than took place in all the marshes, fields, and forests in the country. On any given day, a Noah's Ark trundled in and out of the country. Tropical fish, butterflies, orchids, primates, reptiles; ostrich-skin boots, mink-fur coats, caviar; African hunting trophies—thousands of species passed through Miami every year. Wildlife inspectors cleared those shipments, and like customs inspectors for nature, they were the country's first line of defense against wildlife smuggling. Chances were good that when a special agent had a case to investigate, it was because a wildlife inspector had found something.

Miami International Airport was a sieve for smuggling. Miami's wildlife inspectors were so backed up on paperwork that for a while they'd just given up. For five years nothing got filed. One inspector went crazy, said he could see a fellow agent staring at him through the razor-blade disposal slits inside his hotel medicine cabinet. That inspector went on to work for Mario Tabraue, an animal dealer later sentenced to a hundred years in prison for running a major narcotics operation and dismembering a government informant with a circular saw. Operation Cobra, DEA had called the investigation. Ray Van Nostrand Sr., a reptile wholesaler, had been a key figure in Operation Cobra. Ray was out of prison now and working for his son Mike at a company called Strictly Reptiles.

English knew the odds were good that the tortoises in the courier's suitcase were headed for Strictly Reptiles. No one had ever been able to link Strictly Reptiles or the Van Nostrands to heavy reptile smuggling. Under the federal wildlife laws you had to prove a person receiving an animal *knew* the animal had been smuggled. It would be easier to link a heroin sale in Harlem back to John Gotti. At least with drugs you didn't have to prove a pusher knew cocaine was illegal. The distance between the money and the street was what made stopping a turtle mule at the airport such an easy case to start Bepler on. It would just be Medina; there was no hope of getting anything more.

Bepler stepped out of his house shiny as a new penny. He was six foot four and lean, with dark hair and eyes as blue as the feathers on a hyacinth macaw. He was wearing a pair of khakis, a blue golf shirt, and white tennis sneakers, with a Sig Sauer strapped to his belt. English stifled a laugh. He looked like a freakin' preppy.

The guy Chip was replacing had quit with who knew

how many reptile cases still open. A federal prosecutor was thinking of bringing charges against the agent for leaving his colleagues so desperately in the lurch. And yet it was better to be rid of him. One time he'd flown out to Arizona for in-service training and had left a carful of reptiles to die in the hot sun. Another time he'd broken procedure and had cuffed a suspect with his hands in front instead of in back. Then during the ride to jail, the suspect had thrown his hands over the agent's head and nearly choked him to death with his own handcuffs.

Miami was not a post you asked for, it was a post to which you were sent—like Siberia with mosquitoes and paperwork. One thing was for sure: nobody ever left Miami for greener pastures. You came for reasons that had little to do with career, because you left Miami only one of two ways: fired or retired. Murdered was another way, but that had not happened in a long, long time.

English was still not sure where they were going to assign Bepler. When he'd mentioned something about undercover work and reptiles from his time in New York, she'd laughed out loud. Call it the New Yorker in her, but some things just had to be said.

Chip gave it back to her pretty good, which was the New York way, too. But down deep she was serious. There were stories about the reptile dealers, about drugs and violence—well, she would tell him. Suffice it to say, Miami could be dangerous.

English's specialty was exotic-bird smuggling. She had a soft spot for parrots and was good at using shipping records to take down international bird traffickers. Her husband, Special Agent Terry English, was a Vietnam veteran who liked jumping on an airboat and heading out into the Everglades after armed bad guys. In the service they referred to agents like Terry as "duck cops." They called agents like her "port agents." Being called a duck cop was usually a compliment; being called a port agent often was not. Old-school agents felt that port work was protecting a foreign country's wildlife, which might have been okay if we spent enough money to protect our own.

Anyway, if you were a duck cop you followed the hunting seasons. If you were a port agent you followed the market. During the 1980s the big-ticket item in the wildlife trade was pet birds. Ironically, many believed it was Fred, the cockatoo sidekick on the television crime show *Baretta*, that had fueled the market for illegal birds. English had made psittacines—parrots, cockatoos, and other exotic birds—her specialty. She had just finished a major operation that was yielding prison sentences for bird dealers, collectors, and traffickers all over the United States. To the amazement of the bird world, some of the biggest smugglers to go down were prominent figures in the scientific and conservation communities.

Just as Fred the television bird had spurred a boom in the exotic-bird business and *Jaws* had sparked sales of shark teeth, reptiles had gained a champion in a recent book by Michael Crichton, *Jurassic Park*.

English and Bepler arrived at the airport and proceeded to an examination room, where she introduced him to the customs agents and to Wildlife Inspector Mike Knowles. Carefully they pulled away Medina's laundry to expose the homemade belts of bed linen with hand-sewn pockets containing the tortoises. They began removing the strips of tortoises and lining them up in rows on a long examination counter. Belts of tortoises soon covered an entire wall-length countertop, and still more belts came out of the smuggler's suitcase. In all Medina had packed thirty-four rows, ten baby tortoises to each row, into his luggage, with a few extra tortoises walking about loose.

Customs agents were not pleased with Medina. He had denied having any snakes and had then watched silently as a customs inspector lifted heavy pillowcases out of his suitcase, mistaking them for bags of dirty laundry. Medina confessed to the first bag after it moved, and only when agents began examining further did he confess to the others. Agents pulled three bags of snakes from his luggage and one juvenile boa in a glass jar.

Two pillowcases were swollen with adult Argentine rainbow boas, a slender-bodied cousin of the boa constrictor, eye-catching for the clownlike series of balloons and spots peppering the snake's spine. Compared to the deep reds and purples found in the same species in Brazil, Argentine rainbow boas are a fairly dull mix of browns, but it was not color that gave rainbow boas their name. Their scales have an unusual surface structure made up of closely set microscopic ridges that form a prism, refracting sunlight and giving the snake an astonishing iridescence.

In a third bag agents discovered three newspaper-gray Argentine boas, a species that Argentina considered to be on the verge of extinction.

It was illegal to bring any of these species into the United States without papers.

Bepler read Medina his rights and showed him where to sign to waive them. Medina signed. Then Bepler led

Medina to an interrogation room and handcuffed one of his wrists to the arm of a wooden bench.

English took a chair across from the young man. A producer from the television program *America's Most Wanted* was in town doing a story on a pair of Cuban bird smugglers English had arrested. Jennifer Snell wanted to get some footage of an arrest, so English and Bepler had invited her to film the interrogation.

The agents had no reason to believe it was anything other than an easy case.

"Now, let me understand something," English said in her New York accent. "You were going to keep *three hundred and fifty-seven* of them at your home?"

Medina puffed nervously on a cigarette, chewing slowly at the same time on a piece of gum. Yes, he said.

Bepler pulled a chair close to him and put a sneaker up on the arm of Medina's bench. The total value of the animals Medina had brought in was just under ten grand. Except for the Argentine boas, they were not considered especially endangered animals or even particularly valuable. The quantity was what mattered. Medina's suitcase had contained three hundred forty-seven tortoises and sixteen snakes. To lay off that many animals, Medina had to be bringing them in to somebody big.

Bepler looked Medina over. He was well dressed. His shirt was white; his tie was knotted tightly and held in place with a jeweled clip. He was wearing the big, round eyeglasses that were popular at the moment. He sat with his legs spread wide in a bit of a slouch, but there was no confidence in the young man's demeanor. There was fear.

English suggested to Medina that he could help himself by telling the agents who he was bringing the animals in for.

Instead Medina said that he'd bought the reptiles from a guy named José on Independence Street in Buenos Aires. At his home Medina had a little pool already set up for them. It was his first time. That was the truth, he said. Honest.

"Uh-huh," English said. "If you're afraid of dealing with these people and you tell us that, we can understand that. But if you're telling us that nothing was set up, remember, we've got a lot of contacts. We know a lot of people in the business. It's not gonna take us long to make a few phone calls and get a little background on you. And if what we find out is something other than what you're telling us, then there's no deal..."

Bepler thumbed through Medina's passport. It was bruised with stamps back and forth between Miami and Buenos Aires. Bepler had to look closely to see the dates. He checked twice before he could believe it— Medina had done another trip to Buenos Aires just five days earlier! He turned the page. Medina had also made a trip two weeks before that...and then the week before that...and...

Among his papers, Bepler found a roster sheet from the Dade County Youth Soccer Association, listing boys aged four through eight. The head coach named on the sheet was Tomas Medina. The first player on the team roster was Medina's son. A twenty-seven-year-old married man with a young son. A community coach. A green card.

Who was his buyer?

Bepler got Medina up and led him out of the airport in handcuffs. Then he drove him to jail. As a non–U.S. citizen, Medina was considered a flight risk. He would spend a night behind bars awaiting his bond hearing. As Bepler and English knew well, there was nothing like a night in a cage to help a wildlife smuggler clear his head.

While Medina sat in prison, Bepler looked more carefully through his belongings. The young man had carried with him a day planner. The top entry on the first page of the calendar was in Spanish, but it was not difficult to translate. It read, "Leave at dawn, 6 A.M.," and listed several species of turtles and snakes, with prices in dollars noted beside each one. Below that was an entry concerning a conversation about anacondas and tortoises.

It was not a businessman's diary about computer parts. It was a little black book of his reptile smuggling. Snakes, tortoises, lizards, dates, and dollars—tens of thousands of dollars, tied to trips stretching back more than a year. In the back of the day planner was an address book listing his contacts. One was a prominent Florida herpetologist and educator, another was apparently Medina's true partner in Buenos Aires.

Over and over throughout his calendar Medina had written the name Willie. Willie, it was easy enough to figure out, was Willie Lawson, most recent owner of a wildlife importing company called Pet Farm. For over thirty years, Miami-based Pet Farm had been among the country's leading wholesalers of reptiles, monkeys, and, especially, birds—importing over 30,000 exotic birds a year. If English had wanted to give Bepler a lesson in the history of the South Florida exotic animal business, she could hardly have chosen a better company to use as a case study. Many prominent figures in the animal business had gotten their starts at Pet Farm. The current owner of the popular tourist attraction Parrot Jungle had once owned Pet Farm. Years before, Ray Van Nostrand Sr. had been in charge of Pet Farm's reptile division.

If it were twenty or thirty years earlier, catching a Pet Farm mule would have been a real coup to start Bepler out on. As it was, Pet Farm was hardly much of a player anymore. English was investigating Lawson for smuggling African gray parrots, and the company's reptile division was an anemic version of its former self, outclassed by a new era of reptiles-only mega-importers, notably Strictly Reptiles.

Under subsequent questioning, Medina confessed what the agents already realized: his smuggling was for Pet Farm. But Medina wasn't finished. His smuggling *was* for Pet Farm, he clarified, but his money came from Strictly Reptiles. Bepler asked him to explain what he meant.

According to Medina, when he brought in a suitcase, Pet Farm's reptiles manager, whose name was Dale Marantz, would contact somebody at Strictly Reptiles, and they would issue a check to Marantz, who would cash it and pay Medina. The checks were signed by the owner of Strictly Reptiles, Mike Van Nostrand. Marantz didn't work for Pet Farm, he worked for Van Nostrand; the smuggled reptiles went to Strictly Reptiles, too.

Bepler sat back and laughed. He had a deep laugh that was so loud and genuine, people in restaurants sometimes turned to look. *Pet Farm's reptiles operation was a shell for Strictly Reptiles.* After making his first trip to Miami International Airport and picking up his first reptile mule, Bepler had a little black book, a shipment of smuggled reptiles, and a live witness. He'd known who Mike Van Nostrand was well before he'd transferred to Miami. Stopping Van Nostrand was why Bepler had come.

Operation Cobra

Mike Van Nostrand's grandfather, Raymond, came home from work one day with an earthworm-long cut on the palm of his hand. He'd gotten it at his new job. For years, he had been a machinist for the Arundel dredging company, choosing assignments that meant good fishing—down to Baltimore, up to Portland—dragging his wife, Mary, and their daughter, Vera, along the Atlantic coast with him. Raymond lived for fishing. After eleven years of it, his wife had news for him. "No more fishing," Mary told him. "I'm pregnant again." The year was 1943. The world, of course, was at war. Raymond quit his gypsy fishing life and hired on at a fighter plane manufacturing company close to their Long Island home. Months later, a piece of metal lodged in Raymond's palm. He thought it was nothing, but he awoke soon afterward roiling in a swamp of fever and sweat. The drug penicillin was not yet in common use and his infection turned lethal. Within days, Raymond was dead. Before Mary had even a moment to grieve, their son was born. She gave him the only name that mattered: Raymond.

Soon thereafter, a salesman from John Hancock Mutual Life Insurance came to Mary's door and asked if she was interested. She was not interested in life insurance, she told him, and when she explained why, the salesman filled the uncomfortable silence by asking her if there was anything he could do. There was, she said. He could give her a job.

And so Raymond Van Nostrand came into the world fatherless, and grew up the son of a life insurance saleswoman. His mother did not refer to him as *Ray Jr.* When she cooed to him, and later when she taught him his letters or scolded him, she said her husband's name, *Raymond.* If she was not careful to keep her tone securely boxed, and slipped accidentally from her mother's role, she heard herself speaking the name in a voice she remembered, and then perhaps her husband's face, the fisherman's, returned to her like an echo.

Mary moved from Long Island to New Jersey. She worked her own debit book, selling insurance door to door while an older woman from the neighborhood looked after young Ray. Mary indulged Ray in the one way a single parent struggling to provide for a family can indulge their children: what he cared about he could pursue. And what Ray Van Nostrand cared most about was reptiles.

He was a prodigy.

Before anyone knew it, their house was overrun. His bedroom was filled with aquariums and jars. There were mice in the closet, snake eggs hatching on top of the refrigerator, alligators in the garage. Ray's sister, Vera, would hear sounds in the basement and think it was their father's ghost. On Saturdays, Mary would drive thirteen-year-old Ray up to Suffern, New York, and drop him off at a diner; Ray would hunt the nearby woods day and night, camp out, and be ready for pickup on Sunday loaded with squirming catch. He met a local science teacher who taught him to read scientific journals and doctoral theses to find out where to catch amphibians—what time of year, on what side of which mountain a salamander could be found. He and the teacher then drove to North Carolina and Florida together and caught frogs and salamanders worthy of doctoral research—lots of them—and sold them. Ray caught green tree frogs, wood turtles, water snakes, newts. Newts were popular in fish stores; you could put them in your aquarium. Ray hunted the ponds and puddles of northern New Jersey. He got only a nickel apiece for newts, but in an average morning Ray caught *thousands*. In the spring, before the bell rang for first period, Ray had often pocketed $200.

In the winter of 1958, Ray's Boy Scout troop raised money to pay for a snake-hunting trip to Mexico. Their scoutmaster was Carl Herrmann, who owned Animal Distributors, a company in Queens that imported monkeys, ocelots, reptiles, and other exotic wildlife for zoos and pet stores. Herrmann had connections to the American Museum of Natural History and was close with Carl Kauffeld, the legendary head of herpetology at the Staten Island Zoo, who'd literally written the book on reptile collecting: *Snakes: The Keeper and the Kept,* among other titles.

Kauffeld had the influence on snake enthusiasts that Federal Reserve chairmen have on bankers. A single mention of an interesting species or of a hunting opportunity could alter reptile markets and impact the evolution of a species. In one instance, Kauffeld described an unusually attractive red rat snake (also known as the corn snake) from the Okeetee Hunt Club in Jasper County, South Carolina, inspiring his disciples to rent a bus and travel to the Okeetee property where they reportedly descended with shovels, potato rakes, and crowbars, scouring the area to the bone. Decades later, snake breeders would selectively breed red rat snakes to achieve the "Okeetee look" first discovered by Kauffeld and his friend Carl Herrmann.

Herrmann and two other men drove the Boy Scouts across the United States, and then, from Arizona to Mexico, they began searching for desert tortoises, Gila monsters, and rare Willard's rattlesnakes. Much of the time was spent "road cruising," driving the desert highways in the mornings and evenings, faces stuck from every window like fishing rods, trolling the desert in search of reptiles crossing the road or lolling on the pavement. When not road cruising, the older boys took fifteen-year-old Ray to whorehouses in Nueva Rosita, where they caught geckos and frogs on the walls, and Ray caught an early glimpse of his future. You could have a prostitute in Nueva Rosita for fifty cents. The best women in the house, beautiful women whom top government officials might come to meet, were only ten bucks.

Ray joined the New York and Philadelphia Herpetologists' Societies, organizations for the study and enjoyment of reptiles and amphibians. He gave reptile lectures at his and other local high schools. He took the bus from

Teaneck, then the train to get to the Bronx Zoo, where he worked part-time for the reptile curator, Dr. Herndon Dowling. The boy he replaced had not done a good job cleaning cages or changing water bowls and had also had a bad habit: tying rats to helium-filled balloons and letting them float out over the alligator exhibit, then shooting the balloons with a homemade blow gun. For Ray, working for Dr. Dowling was like a boy interested in rockets getting a job at NASA.

The New York "Herp" club met Saturday mornings at the Bronx Zoo. Afterward you were allowed to sell stuff behind the Heads and Horns building: endangered bog turtles, Madagascar radiated tortoises, venomous snakes. There were no regulations back then—none that were enforced on reptiles, anyway. The Endangered Species Act was more than a decade away. Ray traded snakes with some of the biggest names in herpetology, including Carl Kauffeld and Dr. Dowling.

On one occasion he drove up to the Bronx Zoo with a cobra in a mayonnaise jar for Dr. Dowling. When he looked in the backseat of his car, however, the lid was off the jar, and the cobra was gone. Worse, the car windows were open.

"Where's the cobra?" Dowling asked him.

Ray panicked. He had lost a cobra inside the Bronx Zoo! The first thing he did was call his supplier, Ralph Curtis, in Florida and ask him for another cobra. Then he looked for the venomous snake. Ray's car was a Nash Rambler station wagon, a gigantic hearse of a car that he had dubbed the Pizza Wagon because he used it for his pizza delivery business. Ray lifted up the rear seat and saw the cobra for a moment, but then it was gone down a hole in the car's frame. The Nash Rambler had a unitized body construction, which meant that once the cobra got inside the frame there was no telling where it might come out. Ray had pizzas in the car. He delivered them downtown and then drove to a friend's Amoco station, where he stuck a hose into a hole in the frame and flooded his car with water and ten gallons of bleach. He never found the cobra.

It would be years before he did anything that gave him a rush like that again.

He went on *Name That Tune* as a contestant with an expertise in snakes. The Bergen *Record* gave him a half-page article: "Teaneck Lad Entwined in Hobby of Importing, Selling Snakes." The day the reporter visited, Ray had 5 boa constrictors in his home, 100 iguanas, 150 water snakes, 75 ribbon snakes, 150 turtles, and "other assorted crawling and creeping animals." The reporter described Ray as a "young zoologist" and marveled at his selling 10,000 reptiles and amphibians a year while still only a teenager. A photograph accompanying the article shows Ray holding a boa constrictor while his mother looks on. Ray is smiling, his hair slicked back like Elvis Presley's. His mother has the patient and unflappable look of a nurse. Behind them, a shotgun hangs on a pegboard wall.

Ray's stepfather, Edward Kerr, added his two cents about Ray's hobby: "It's all right so long as he keeps them inside. I don't want them running around." One of Ray's turtles had recently fallen into his stepfather's cocktail glass. "He was stewed," Ray joked.

Ray told the reporter he hoped to study zoology at the University of Southern California and that he wanted to get his master's in herpetology. In actuality, Ray had no serious plans for college. He was making $500 in a day selling newts and baby turtles.

He ordered the baby turtles from Papa Gooch "the Turtleman," in Tiptonville, Tennesee, and from the Strange family turtle farm in Jonesville, Louisiana, for a dime apiece. He added a few pennies to the price and sold tens of thousands of baby turtles to E.J. Korvette and Carl Herrmann's Animal Distributors in New York, who sold them to Hartz Mountain, which supplied canaries and other live pets to Woolworth, Macy's, Sears Roebuck, W. T. Grant, S. S. Kresge, John Wanamaker's, and others.

Ray was born into the gilded age for the American pet business, a time when virtually anything alive could legally be loaded onto a boat or an airplane, health and conservation rules were still frail, and wild animals were popular novelties. In 1954, Wanamaker's opened an animal division in its department store, including orangutans and chimpanzees and even a glass-enclosed baby elephant beside ordinary puppies and kittens. Wild animal dealer Henry Trefflich supplied the store. Especially around Christmastime, Macy's was alive with parakeets, canaries, and finches, released from its fourth-floor pet department "to give the store atmosphere." Interior decorators in Manhattan accessorized homes and corporate offices with live birds—not as pets, but to enhance their color schemes. New aquarium technologies, such as power filters, heaters, and medication, spawned growth in the tropical fish industry. Baby turtles sold by the tens of millions.

You could always sell baby turtles. The markup retailers applied was unbelievable. Adding in a cheap lagoon bowl and a shaker of dried ant pupae, any retailer had itself the pizza of the pet business: flour, water, tomatoes, cheese, and the rest was all profit. It is a maxim of the pet industry that you can sell anything you can fit in a cage. There was something special, Ray discovered, about the color green. People went nuts for it. Too early in his life to realize it, he had fused green animals with green money, and before long he would be chasing the latter into some very dark places.

After a fight with his stepfather, Ray dropped out of high school and ran down to Florida to stay with wild animal dealer Ralph Curtis, the man who'd supplied him with many of his imported reptiles. Curtis owned a wildlife importing company in Hollywood called Wild Cargo.

When Ray showed up at Curtis's home without warning, Curtis chuckled, shaking his head. "I was wondering when you'd get here," he said.

Ray was surprised. "You were expecting me?"

"Sure. Your mother called and said you might be headed this way."

Mary knew her son. There was nothing she could do to keep Ray at home. And she herself was liking her second husband less and less. She asked Curtis to look after Ray. Curtis did, and after a year of working at Wild Cargo, Ray returned home and finished high school. Before he left, he gave Curtis a good deal on a very clean-smelling Nash Rambler.

Ray met a younger girl named Elaine Pacerno who wasn't anything like him, at least not on the surface. She liked literature and music, but she also enjoyed the adventure of skipping high school for a day to hunt newts with Ray. After high school Elaine enrolled in Villanova University and Ray bought a pet shop in the Bronx. Everything Ray touched turned to gold. He had a pizza delivery business, and an international reptile business. He owned a few cars, and he had done it all on his own. Within a year, Ray and Elaine married, and at Ray's insistence, Elaine dropped out of college.

For their honeymoon, Ray took Elaine down to Ralph Curtis's. If that wasn't bad enough, he asked her to drop him off in the middle of the Everglades so he could go snake hunting. She almost divorced him right then. Instead, they had a son they named Raymond, and then the following year had a second son. They named him Michael.

Ray's pet store was called Bronx Park Pets; it was located across the street from the Bronx Zoo. The owners had been customers of his and were famous for their birdseed. They not only gave Ray a good price on the store, but also threw in the secret of their birdseed: anise oil. By adding a little anise oil to the seed, you hooked the birds, as if on a narcotic. Once a parakeet got a taste for anise, it often refused its regular food. Exasperated bird customers from Brooklyn traveled all the way back to the Bronx just to buy the birdseed at Bronx Park Pets.

Everyone who took the subway to the Bronx Zoo passed by the big glass windows of Ray's pet shop. He sold squirrel monkeys, mynah birds, and marmosets for $14.95 each. Capuchin monkeys were $59.95. A chimpanzee was $500. He sold jaguars and tigers. Ocelots were in vogue. The Long Island Ocelot Club was expanding the number of species its members could keep to include margays, cheetahs, and pumas. Puerto Ricans from the local neighborhood bought monkeys. Voodoo practitioners bought monkey dung. On Saturdays Ray would take a whole box of his most flea-bitten parakeets, frail birds too mangy to fly, and dump them out in the park next to the zoo. Then all weekend long he would ring up sales to people wanting cages and seed for the escaped parakeet they caught from the zoo. Dry goods were everything.

Neighborhood children would come in with a toad or a box turtle and he would buy it and then point them across the street to the Bronx River to catch more. One boy in particular turned up over and over again with jars of newts Ray bought for a nickel apiece. Ray would send him back out and the kid, whose name was Alfred Ojeda, would return as thrilled by the adventure as if the Bronx River were the Amazon. Many of the truly exotic animals Ray sold came from his old Boy Scout leader Carl Herrmann. Others he shipped up from Ralph Curtis at Wild Cargo.

At the time, New York was still a major location for companies supplying America's zoos and natural history museums. Ray got to know the country's once-great animal importers like Frederik Zeehandelaar, the Louis Ruhe family, and Henry Trefflich, "the Monkey King," on Fulton Street. In his lifetime, Trefflich imported over 1.5 million monkeys and thousands of apes. He supplied NASA with the pioneering chimpanzee Ham and the rhesus monkey Able. He sold Jonas Salk the rhesus monkeys for his polio vaccine research, for which Franklin D. Roosevelt intervened personally on Trefflich's behalf to enable him to bypass a World War II trade embargo. Monkeys were a big item because of the government's research (the National Foundation for Infantile Paralysis alone purchased an estimated eight thousand monkeys a year). Cheetah of the Tarzan movies was a Trefflich sale. The title of Trefflich's first autobiography was *They Never Talk Back*; his second book was *Jungle for Sale*.

For reasons forgotten, the city gave Ray $2,700 to take

over his building. Ray left his own pet store behind and got a job running the pet-shop concession at Blumstein's department store on 125th Street in Harlem. The owner of the concession, Jerry Margolis, was a retailing genius. It was Margolis who taught Ray, among other things, how to turn a pet-shop lemon into lemonade. These were retailing lessons Ray would use throughout his life—in the pet business, in the gun business, and in the narcotics business.

For example, parakeets with poor feathers were cheaper than parakeets in good condition. Margolis bought the runts late out of the egg, as well as others with feather problems so bad breeders called them "runners," because they couldn't fly. He paid thirty-five cents apiece for the runners, renamed them bobtail parakeets, and sold them for a buck. The line would stretch outside onto the street—for deformed parakeets! Parakeet customers also bought cages. And they bought Ray's magical birdseed.

Margolis gave fish tanks away to sell fish, and then he sold the fish-tank filter and pump kits...and the water heaters...and the fish food...and the gravel...and the pH test kits...and then the replacement fish...and, for some, the more advanced fish.

The pet business was recession proof. The sick and the elderly would feed their pets before they fed themselves. Ray got involved in some half a dozen pet ventures in the New York area, including a stint with the legendary Vic Hritz, the owner of the Crystal Aquarium, at Ninety-third Street and Third Avenue on the Upper East Side, pet shop to such stars as Allen Funt, Rosemary Clooney, Anthony Quinn, and a young John Kennedy Jr. (who later worked for a summer at the Bronx Zoo's Reptile House). Ray went into the bird business with Margolis; he opened a discount tropical fish store in Tappan, New York. And then Ray made a decision that would change his family forever. The next phase of Ray's life began with a rare, petroleum-blue snake, and ended in murder and a federal trial.

In a Florida not yet dominated by Disney World, the tourist industry centered on exotic animals, especially reptiles. Parrot Jungle, Monkey Jungle, Ross Allen's Reptile Institute, and the Miami Serpentarium were all enormously popular tourist destinations, as were the Seminole Indians' alligator wrestling shows and a thousand roadside zoos. The 1960s television series *Tarzan* had put Americans in a jungle frame of mind; *Flipper* and *Gentle Ben* added to the image of Florida as a place torn from the pages of Kipling's *Jungle Book*. The only tropical "island" Americans can drive to, Florida had it all. And even if it didn't, it still had one species few other states had.

Just as a trip to Africa was not complete without seeing a lion or a hippopotamus, a trip to Florida was in some way a failure without seeing that king of all that is primordial, the American alligator. Pink flamingos were beautiful, and manatees were dumbfounding, but it took an alligator to know you were in Florida. When Ray first traveled to the state as a teenager, souvenir shops had sold live baby alligators; you ordered them from the cashier and then received yours weeks later in the mail, packaged in a cardboard tube (often from Ralph Curtis's Wild Cargo). Banks gave baby alligators away to new customers; tourist traps sold them stuffed as toys. They sold alligator toenail necklaces and alligator-foot back scratchers, too. Boutiques sold alligator handbags. The University of Florida mascot was, of course, an alligator.

As a commodity, the alligator was priceless for the tourism industry. But for the pet industry, Florida's most valuable reptile was the snake. Snake hunting, which really meant snake collecting, was a viable profession in those days, and Florida was a snake hunter's paradise. The entire state dripped color. Scarlet kingsnakes—red, ivory, and black mimics of the venomous coral snake—hunted anoles and other lizards at the base of palm trees. Tiger-striped Florida kingsnakes warmed themselves on country roads. Yellow rat snakes roped through Australian pine trees. Red rat snakes hid under logs and old tin lying along most any highway. By far the most impressive snake of all was the eastern indigo snake, the largest nonvenomous snake in the United States, and increasingly rare.

Yellow rat snakes sold for thirty-five cents a foot. Reds were sixty-five cents a foot. Indigos were protected under Florida law, and illegal to collect. Around Lake Okeechobee, a good snake hunter could catch thirty reds in a day, giving him a modest $400 a week on just one species, and a life in the outdoors. Plenty of men eked out a living selling cheap snakes like these by the foot. Ray wanted to be a professional snake hunter, but he had no intention of living like one.

The indigo snake was black gold in the pet trade. A good specimen, smuggled out of Florida, might sell for $250 in New York. Indigos were massive purple monsters. Hailed as good pets in even the most basic pet-shop snake book, they were as docile as they were large. You could find a seven-footer laid out in a culvert and pick it up by the middle of its body without fear. They did not bite, a reason they had long been favored by erotic snake dancers in the days of the traveling carnival. They ate everything. Ray would be looking up in tree branches for rat snakes and suddenly notice an indigo beside him, looking up in the tree branches for snakes, too. They ate turtles and fish. Once Ray saw one eat a rock.

Eastern indigos were one of the first reptiles in the United States to receive government protection. Along with Florida, Mississippi and Georgia also protected the snake. Catching or selling an indigo in any of those states was illegal, but that did not stop people out of state from buying them. Indigos were rare, but they were not rare everywhere. One of the few places they could still be found was on Florida's east coast, outside of a city called Fort Pierce.

Ray moved his wife and sons to Fort Pierce, and bought himself a motorcycle, a Suzuki TS-185 with saddlebags for carrying pillowcases and tree-climbing gear. He intended to make indigos his specialty. Elaine, who got her degree at Fairleigh Dickinson, found a job teaching English.

Indigo hunting paid well. Ray was catching five indigos a day, easily. His record was twenty-three. He dug up their eggs by the score, took them home to hatch, and sold the babies. He had so many indigos in his yard that one time when he was away state wildlife officers discovered his cache and wanted to arrest Elaine. Ray lost most of his snakes that time, but getting caught was nothing really. The penalties in-state were minor, and the federal law that prohibited interstate transportation of a state's protected wildlife had a flaw. To prosecute, the feds had to prove your snakes were from one of the protected states. To get around the law, all an indigo poacher had to do was tell the feds the snakes in question had come from either Alabama or South Carolina. Nobody had seen an indigo in those two states in years, but records did exist of their being found there, and so the failure of just two states to protect indigos fueled a black market across the United States and overseas, too.

Most of what Ray caught he sent north, especially to New York. Just thirty-two years old, Ray had almost twenty years of pet industry contacts built up. To him, indigos were man-made snakes. You couldn't find them in the wild. They were attracted to where man had destroyed the wild. Ray and other hunters termed the pump houses on citrus and sugarcane plantations "snake traps" because you could find them so easily there.

For other species, Ray scavenged carpet remnants and sheets of plywood and dropped them along forest edges and at the ends of sugarcane drainage ditches. Snake hunters call these traps "sets"; they work by giving mice a dark place to build nests and snakes a dark place to eat mice. In Florida snakes were so plentiful that if you gave them a cool place to hide, odds were good they'd be there waiting for you. When Ray checked his sets, money crawled out.

By the time he moved to Florida, his mentor Ralph Curtis had closed Wild Cargo and so Ray sold the legal reptiles he caught to Pet Farm, the wildlife company owned then by a veterinarian named Dr. Bern Levine. Most of the professional snake hunters in South Florida took their snakes to Pet Farm. Ray made a good living selling to Pet Farm, but he was not impressed with the staff there and told Dr. Levine he could do better.

Dr. Levine, whose own interests leaned toward orang-utans and exotic birds, accepted Ray's challenge. He put Ray in charge of Pet Farm's reptile operations, but his terms were strict: Ray would receive no salary and would have to hire and pay his own people. In return, Ray would be allowed to keep 10 percent of anything he sold. His first year, Ray sold a million dollars' worth of reptiles. He made a hundred grand.

Hunting reptiles in Florida is a twice-a-day job. Mornings you get up early to catch the snakes as they come out of their dens to warm up in the new sun. Evenings you catch them trying to absorb the last of the day's heat, often at the edges of asphalt roads. You could catch lizards in the evenings, too. There are seasonal animals like anoles, the tiny green or brown lizards often sold as American chameleons. Full moons are no good. Rain is no good. It is an easy life.

Working inside a place on Pet Farm's scale was a different story. Ray's days were spent packing boxes for shipment: turtles and snakes and lizards and frogs; birds and monkeys, too. Levine had a pet chimp named Debbie, and when he wasn't around the veteran employees would give Debbie a cup of coffee and a cigarette and then hide out and smoke and drink coffee with her.

The animal business is a lint screen for human vices. You do not have to go far to find somebody into any crime you can think of. Ask any animal dealer or pet-shop owner who the worst among them are and they will always give you the same answer: *the reptile guys.*

One day Dr. Levine discovered that his baby jaguar

was missing. Immediately he accused the reptile men of stealing his cat, and when they denied it Levine brought in a polygraph expert to give his people a lie detector test. When the expert finished his testing, he gave Dr. Levine his report: all of his staff were stealing from him; they were all doing drugs; but none of them had stolen his baby jaguar.

Ray had trouble keeping up with the action. When he arrived in Florida he did not drink or take drugs. He was no saint, but he hadn't tried drugs. Still, after packing boxes for shipment late into the night three days straight, with little sleep, Ray found himself flagging.

"Here, Ray," a coworker said, "try this."

Ray discovered amphetamines. He discovered cocaine. It was the late 1970s and everybody had at least one toe in the drug business. To Ray, drugs were just something a little dangerous that you picked up and sold—familiar territory. He took to the drug business the same way he'd taken to reptiles.

One day a young man appeared at Pet Farm. "I want to buy a tiger," the man told Dr. Levine. He was maybe twenty-seven, open shirt, cowboy boots, gold chains, the new high-end Mercedes 450SEL. A Miami Cuban (with a bit of Lebanese ancestry) wanting to buy a tiger—it wasn't hard to figure out Mario Tabraue's line of work.

Dr. Levine turned his back on Tabraue, but not before pointing a finger toward Ray. "Go see that guy over there," he said.

Tabraue was not just any drug dealer. He was "chairman of the board" of the Tabraue syndicate, a $79 million drug-smuggling operation, "one of South Florida's most prolific and violent drug gangs," according to the *Miami*

Herald. Tabraue and his father owned Miami cops. They owned politicians. Mario was untouchable. He lived in a Coconut Grove mansion. He was so much like Al Pacino's character Tony Montana in the movie *Scarface*—the mountains of cocaine, the machine guns, the mirrored ceilings, even the monogrammed leather chairs—that when Ray, who got Tabraue his tiger, saw the movie, he exclaimed, "Look! They even got Mario's chair!" The men's initials were just reversed, and Ray was sure Oliver Stone had consulted Tabraue for the script.

Along with drugs, Tabraue ran an exotic-animal business called Zoological Imports, one of the country's premier animal-importing companies. His father had been a part of Brigade 2506, U.S.-backed heroes of the Bay of Pigs invasion. Now Guillermo Tabraue operated a jewelry store in Miami's Little Havana: a clearinghouse, the government believed, for his other interests, too.

Mario Tabraue had started in the pet business in high school, working after school in Miami at a pet shop called Henry's Tropical Fish, learning to breed and sell their stock. When he became an adult, Tabraue's favorite species were big cats and monkeys. He was gifted in their care, and he also kept a menagerie of leopards, monkeys—even a giraffe—at his home. One day, while Ray was setting up Tabraue's turtle pond, he saw couriers shouldering duffel bags of cash into Tabraue's home. He went inside to find what he guessed was $7 million spread out on the floor. Another time he brought Tabraue a rare tortoise. Tabraue turned to his wife and asked, "You like this? You do?" He set the tortoise down and Ray watched a $500 animal disappear across the lawn.

They began to work together. At first it wasn't doing

drugs that hooked Ray. During the *Miami Vice* years anybody in South Florida with a boat or a house on the water had a ready-made side business just unloading. Ray had a boat, and he still had lots of friends in New York.

He borrowed $18,000 from his mother and bought a silver Grumman step van to deliver reptiles as part of a reptile wholesale company he called Repfibia. Tabraue would look out his window and say, "Here comes Ray in his SWAT truck." The van had a roof-mounted air conditioner, important for keeping reptiles cool in the Florida sun. Ray took the filters out and used the air conditioner to deliver guns and cocaine.

"I need three cockatoos," Ray might say on the telephone, and Tabraue would know Ray was on his way to pick up three kilos of cocaine. "Three lesser-crested cockatoos" meant three ounces.

All the big drug dealers were collectors of some kind. When they saw a car they liked, or an animal they liked, or knives or guns or commemoratives, or Krugerrands— they just bought them, with cash. They would say, *Ray, can you get me this?*

Ray believed he had pirate blood in him. There was just something that pointed him in directions a pirate would go, and, like his father, he was drawn to the ocean. He considered Jimmy Buffett's "A Pirate Looks at Forty" his theme song.

In addition to exotic animals, Ray got these big dealers guns. Walther PPKs, Browning High-Powers, Smith & Wessons, MAC-10s, MAC-11s, M-16s, silencers. His sources for many of the guns were ex-cops he met at gun shows.

He was doing a couple of grams of coke and a fistful of quaaludes a day back then. He would drive around with guns in his car, get to a dealer's home, and throw open the trunk: "Hey, look what I got!"

He started his own drug business. He began with marijuana he picked up from Tabraue and others in 100- to 200-pound lots. Then, the year his son Mike turned twelve, Ray moved up from marijuana to cocaine. Prices for cocaine at the time were hovering just over $20,000 per kilogram. At his peak Ray sold five to six kilos of cocaine a month, directly and as a distributor with outlets around the country.

He employed retailing techniques he'd learned in the pet business. He sent guys out to Nebraska to pick hemp growing wild along the highway, then used it to cut the marijuana he was selling. He called it Hamburger Helper. When Fat Cuban Ricky's cocaine laboratory blew up and got drywall dust and smoke in Mario Tabraue's cocaine, Ray sold it as Gray Ghost. The cocaine tasted all right, but customers could not get past the idea of snorting something that even Ray agreed looked like two-day-old New York City snow, so Ray gave away free samples.

Soon he was phoning Tabraue. "I need more of those Gray Ghost cockatiels," he said. It worked well—Ray sold four or five kilos in three months—but then Ray took some Gray Ghost on an airplane flight to San Francisco, and for some reason the cabin pressure or altitude turned his Gray Ghost pink. When he landed, Ray stepped out of the plane with a new product: Pink Panther. It was a hell of a lot easier to sell than Gray Ghost.

Tabraue chuckled. *Ray could sell a healthy man a casket!*

Ray suggested that Tabraue add a reptile division to Zoological Imports. Though Tabraue was horrified by even a tiny anole lizard, he agreed. To overcome his fears, Tabraue encouraged Ray to buy the best, with a particular push for white animals. Ray bought albino rattlesnakes and albino monocled cobras. Tabraue acquired some of Tom Crutchfield's first albino Burmese pythons. Mr. Dang in Thailand was such a good source for white species, Tabraue named his albino macaque Mr. Dang.

Echoing the sporadic nature of his pet business during his years in New York, Ray's businesses moved frequently. He was constantly changing buildings and partners, following opportunity. He left Pet Farm and worked for a time at a store called Royal Pet Supply, until he was caught selling supplies to Tabraue out of the back of the store. Ray sold reptiles for Tabraue at Zoological Imports, he sold them out of his own warehouse, and he sold them out of his step van. Ray hired his main cocaine buyer from Philadelphia as an assistant, a man named Bob Udell, who prior to moving to Florida had run the reptile department in a large Philadelphia pet store. Before that Udell had been a defendant in *U.S. v. Molt,* the reptile-smuggling case that had drawn the attention of President Jimmy Carter. After a disagreement with Tabraue, Ray relocated his reptile business to his family's garage. He called his company Ray's Reptiles. He conducted his drug business from there, too.

Ray's wife, Elaine, considered leaving him, taking the boys and running, but what was there to do? She was not a partner in her husband's piracy. She had loved their adventures together in high school, racing cars and cutting class to hunt newts, Ray as the precocious darling of New York zoo curators and teachers, pockets full of money from any challenge he took on—Ray was someone you read about.

There was no stopping Ray, no pulling him in off the ocean the way Mary had done with his father years ago. And, for all of his dark crimes, Ray was not a dark or evil man. He seemed to be obeying something inherited. Elaine, too, believed he had pirate blood in him. We don't recognize pirates anymore. We see murderers and thieves on the news; we see entertaining swashbucklers in the movies. Our only pirate terms are saved for Wall Street, "corporate raiders" and "hostile takeovers," for example. Surely the 1980s junk-bond traders in wool-blend suits were not the best America could do when it came to pirates. And any pirate who espied the wonder at hand in 1980s Florida—a tropical paradise teeming with flesh, guns, snakes, and cocaine—would have set his course and followed it.

Ray sailed from pet business to drug opportunity, laughing and partying with murderers and thieves, showering his wife and boys with presents on his return.

He slipped further out of control. That time the cobra had gotten loose in his car had been a rush, and ever since that day he had been chasing after a rush like that without looking where he was headed. In the pot days everyone was happy, more or less; quaaludes were a mellow drug, too. But cocaine was bad news, and then the market started freebasing. People began killing people. In Miami, the so-called "cocaine cowboys" were machine-gunning people in broad daylight. When Ray heard Mario arguing on the telephone with some Colombians, his first thought was "How many caimans do I have in the back?" A caiman is an alligator from Central or South America, and a good way to get rid of anything with meat on it.

The end began the day Ray swung into a friend's driveway behind the wheel of a Silver Anniversary Trans Am he had just had modified. A switch on the dash made the license plate roll over; other switches caused nails and oil to drop from compartments welded into the car's underbody. The rear taillights opened to expose MAC-10 machine guns. He had not yet installed the machine guns. He didn't want the car for himself. Drug dealers liked the next shiny toy, and it was hard to find something shiny and new when they drove bulletproof Mercedeses and ordered out thousand-dollar lunches from the Forge. Ray had taken something fairly ordinary and spruced it up—he'd turned a cheap car into a bobtail parakeet. He planned to sell his James Bond car to a drug dealer, but instead he pulled right into the middle of a drug bust.

He had a Walther PPK in his cowboy boot, and a little blow and some quaaludes in the car. The bust was part of a Florida investigation into Tabraue called Operation Giraffe. Investigators seized more than six tons of marijuana, but their case relied on some questionable wiretaps and was thrown out. Tabraue got Ray a lawyer, and Ray walked away from the Trans Am stunt with a fine.

But on December 16, 1987, Raymond Van Nostrand was arrested again, this time in connection with a drug sale that a courier of his had made to a bird dealer in Fort Worth, Texas, three years earlier. It was a relatively small matter. Even federal prosecutor Steven Chaykin would admit that he did not care about Ray's cocaine sales or about parrots in Texas. Chaykin did not care about Ray at all.

Chaykin wanted the Tabraue narcotics organization, which the federal government believed was responsible for over $100 million in narcotics trafficking, the bribing of police and political figures throughout South Florida and Key West, and the murder of at least two people. To make their RICO case, the government needed someone who'd known Mario Tabraue over the life of his criminal enterprise. In the government's eyes, Ray had the power to send Mario Tabraue to prison for the rest of his life.

Ray refused to talk. He went to trial for the Texas cocaine business, his jury deadlocked, and he went free. Chaykin tried him again on related charges the very next week. Ray was so out of control he was doing cocaine in the courthouse bathroom. His son Mike was sitting in the courtroom. Three days later a jury convicted Ray on all counts. The government told him he was facing decades of prison time. His lawyer said he could go away for life. This time, Ray agreed to testify against Mario Tabraue.

Ten years after Ray and Tabraue met at Pet Farm, Chaykin stood up in federal court and declared the results of Operation Cobra: "Ladies and gentlemen, what this trial is about is drugs, money, murder, and corruption. It is not about whales, it is not about animals taken into captivity, it is not about parakeets, it is not about birds. Drugs, money, murder, and corruption . . ."

Chaykin accused the Tabraue organization of smuggling 500,000 pounds of marijuana and "hundreds of kilograms of cocaine," and murder. According to court testimony, when Tabraue's associates discovered a government informant named Larry Nash in their midst, they shot him in the head. Then they brought his body to Tabraue, who tried to cut his head off with a machete, failed, then took a circular saw, dismembered Nash, threw his body parts into a horse trough with a dozen bags of charcoal and an abundance of lighter fluid, and barbecued him. On February 6, 1981, Tabraue's wife, Maria, was shot nine times and killed. Prosecutors alleged that Tabraue had ordered his wife's murder after she'd threatened to go to the authorities about his drug business.

In December 1988, the United States government called Raymond Van Nostrand Sr. to the witness stand. Mario Tabraue seethed as Ray described their history together. In the middle of Ray's testimony, Tabraue jumped to his feet. "You're just a fat, lying, son-of-a-bitch rat!" he screamed. At the end of the trial, a jury found Tabraue guilty on every major count except his wife's murder. His father, Guillermo Tabraue, was granted a mistrial after the shocking revelation that he had secretly worked as a high-level informant for a covert DEA-CIA narcotics operation run by Lt. Col. Lucien Conein, CIA's man at the center of the overthrow and assassination of South Vietnamese President Ngo Dinh Diem.

Snakes, pot, cocaine, guns, CIA, Vietnam—the more the government tugged at South Florida, the further the world seemed to unravel.

Judge James W. Kehoe sentenced Mario Tabraue to one hundred years in prison. Kehoe assumed it would be a life sentence, but Tabraue proved to be very knowledgeable when it came to crime in the international wildlife and drug worlds. He would cooperate with the government, be out in just over a decade, and would return to the exotic wildlife business. Ray was sentenced to five years. To protect him from Tabraue, Ray was assigned to a witness security (WITSEC) unit in Phoenix.

In prison Ray met some men at least as dangerous as any he knew on the outside. Men with multiple murders...Nicky Scarfo's mob from Philadelphia...the Pizza Connection guys, New York mobsters who famously used pizza shops as fronts for their heroin ring. One guy was in for killing a federal judge. Ray met Hell's Angels and Mexican mafia. WITSEC was for government witnesses who feared for their lives. Some of the men were testifying against organizations so powerful they were afraid their former associates might send a missile into the prison and blow up the whole complex. Nobody used names. They called Ray "Snake." Ray told them about the reptile business in Miami. Some guys with money had no idea what they were going to do when they got out. Ray said to them, "Hey, you want to go into the reptile business?"

Reptile Love

When Ray Van Nostrand was thirteen years old, Dr. Karl Patterson Schmidt of the Field Museum, "the dean of American herpetologists," demonstrated that even the best reptile men make mistakes.

On September 25, 1957, Dr. Schmidt entered the office of the Field Museum's reptiles curator, who was holding an unusual African snake in one hand while looking it up in a key with the other. Dr. Schmidt had started his career by researching African reptiles, and after many years he had just recently returned to that very topic. He grabbed the snake—slightly too far behind the head, as he quickly acknowledged—and was bitten on the left thumb.

After the snake was "disengaged," he and the other men agreed that it was a venomous African boomslang. Schmidt was a scientist, and he could not resist documenting his experience, intending to record his story from bite to recovery. It was a small specimen, rear-fanged, and hardly worth bothering about. Only one of the snake's fangs had caught Schmidt, piercing three millimeters into the fleshy part of his thumb. The wound had bled freely and Schmidt, aged sixty-seven and healthy, had augmented the flow by immediately and vigorously sucking his injured digit.

A half hour later, Schmidt noticed a bluish dot one centimeter in diameter on the tip of his thumb. "Look," he said, "I've got a local reaction." The embarrassed herpetologist took the suburban train to the house he shared with his wife in Homewood, feeling nauseated.

By evening Schmidt had a strong chill, a temperature of 101.7 degrees, and was shaking. There was blood in his mouth—leakage, he knew, from the thin capillary walls in his gums. Schmidt had been educated at Cornell, had worked at the American Museum of Natural History, and had left thirty-five years earlier to found the herpetology department at the Field Museum, eventually rising to chief curator of zoology.

Dr. Schmidt ate two pieces of milk toast and went to bed at 9:00. For three hours he slept well. At 12:20 he awoke and made his way to the toilet to urinate. He produced only a very small amount of fluid, which appeared to him to be mostly blood. He looked in the mirror and saw dried blood at both corners of his mouth, from which he concluded that he had bled steadily from the time he had gone to sleep. He belched repeatedly to try to relieve the pain in his belly. At 4:00 A.M., after a fitful sleep, he took an enema, as he had not moved his bowels the previous day.

He then drank a glass of water, which caused him to violently vomit the contents of his supper. He felt much better afterward and slept well until 6:30 A.M., at which time he awoke and found his temperature was consistent with his sleep: it was 98.2 and progressing back toward normal. Gratified, he ate a bowl of cereal, a poached egg on toast, applesauce, and drank his morning coffee.

"After breakfast," Clifford H. Pope wrote in the herpe-tological journal *Copeia*, "Dr. Schmidt was up and active. In fact, he felt so well at about 10 o'clock that he telephoned to the Museum to expect him at work the next day."

According to Schmidt's diary, he had only a slight bleeding from the bowels after breakfast. He produced no urine, but instead put out an ounce or so of blood every three hours rather than the several ounces of urine he nor-mally expelled. His mouth and nose continued to bleed. "Not excessively," he noted optimistically.

Pope, who had for years been Schmidt's right hand and had retired from the Field Museum not long before to write popular reptile books, continues:

> He got up to eat at noon but vomited after lunch and soon began to have difficulty in breathing. This grew worse until his labored efforts could be heard all over the house. At the onset of these alarming symp-toms, Mrs. Schmidt called the inhalator squad and the family physician. Attempts at resuscitation at first brought warmth back to Dr. Schmdit's hands and normal color to his face, but his restoral was of short duration. He was transported to the hospital where he arrived shortly before 3:00 P.M. and was promptly pronounced dead from respiratory paralysis.

His autopsy, performed the next morning at 9:30 by a Cook County, Illinois, coroner's physician, revealed mas-sive hemorrhages in his intestines. Small and multiple hemorrhages were found in his brain, as well as in the walls of his heart and his lungs. Death was ascribed, wrote Pope, "to cerebral hemorrhages caused by 'venom from the snake bite.'"

It might as easily have been ascribed to love.

~~~~

"Foul and loathsome" Linnaeus called reptiles and amphibians. "Creeping thing" is our Greek root for their study: herpetology. In serpent form reptiles are Satan himself. Snakes are the most widely dreamed about, most feared, most religiously significant creature in the world. A squiggle, they are believed to be the first animal ever drawn. As sea serpents they embodied terra incognita on ancient maps; they marked a "Don't Tread on Me" barrier between the colonies and the rest of the world; they are the physical line between the Judeo-Christian notions of good and evil. No other creature figures so widely in folklore and myth. No other creature is so universally accused of hijacking the amygdala, the region of the brain responsible for flight. According to a recent hypothesis published in the *Journal of Human Evolution,* the shape of the human head—eyes front, large brain—stems from a desire by man's ancestors to avoid snake predators.

Powerful John D. Rockefeller was terrified of them. Harvard's E. O. Wilson offers them as the exception to prove his rule that man is genetically "biophilic" and needs wildlife around him to be happy. Even jungle-saint Albert Schweitzer, winner of the Nobel Prize for his "reverence for life" philosophy, carried a rifle for ministering to snakes.

And yet, basking in the sunlight of religion, myth, and

folktale—frameworks that define what it is to be human—
can be found an inordinate number of hardworking reptiles. In Hindu legend, the earth is supported by four
elephants standing on a turtle's back. A cobra spread its
hood to protect Gautama, hero of Buddhism. The serpent
in the Garden of Eden represented Satan, but it was also
the catalyst for man's redemption. In many cases, reptiles
are considered both good and bad: God sent down fiery
serpents to afflict the children of Israel, but Moses picked
one up to heal them.

Healing and protection are long-standing themes for
the serpent: the wand of Asclepius, Greek god of medicine, wrapped by a single serpent, inspires the symbols of
the American Medical Association and the World Health
Organization. Hermes' winged staff, entwined by a pair of
snakes, forms the caduceus, a symbol of alchemy and commerce, and a second symbol of medicine. Jung considered
ouroboros, the snake swallowing its own tail, to be the one
archetypal symbol that explained absolutely everything.

In *The Frog Prince,* a beautiful princess drops her
golden ball into a deep spring and must allow a frog
into her bedroom to get it back, maturing thereby into a
woman. Fairy tales and myth often place an odd creature
on the path of the hero to signal an opportunity exists:
turn right for good or left for evil. Of all the harbingers
of change in fairy tales and myth—disfigured dwarfs,
shriveled witches, even Yoda—it is reptiles (and amphibians) that are considered ugly enough without embellish-
ment to awaken the part of the brain that listens to fairy
tales. In real life, it is possible that reptiles have the power
to switch off a person's thinking brain and switch on the
subconscious, opening the door to a person's most deeply

suppressed passions. Perhaps this is what makes reptiles so terrifying.

Coiled at the center of the *Oxford English Dictionary*'s definition of the word *fascinate* is this: "of a serpent." Evolved from lizards, deliverers of venom—snakes are the villains of the animal kingdom. And yet, throughout history, snakes have been recognized for their power to bewitch man, to deprive him of resistance, to draw him near.

What explains our fascination? Why would a man as intelligent as Dr. Schmidt make reptiles, snakes in particular, his life's work, and his death's last pursuit? Why will monkeys terrified of even a snakelike piece of garden hose nevertheless return for a life-threatening second peek?

Fascination is in part the allure of the circus freak, the deformity that attracts not only as something unusual but also as something that amplifies the perfection of our own bodies. The two-headed fetus swimming in a jar of formaldehyde makes us feel beautiful, psychologists say. Slithering movements, flickering tongues, scaly skin, lidless eyes—snakes are the opposite of *Homo sapiens*. They are alien. It is possible that they make us feel more human.

Psychologists note that collecting is a way of compensating for lack of control. In Freudian language, it is an adult manifestation of the anal retentive, the child collecting fecal control over his parents. What we collect is thought to reflect something specific to our childhood experience. Everyone "collects" something—mementos, books, recipes. To collect nothing at all requires an act of monastic will.

The sixteenth- and seventeenth-century *Wunderkammern,* the wonder closets of the well-to-do, were not complete without dried reptiles; stuffed crocodiles, tortoise shells, and gigantic python skins were highly prized (along with armadillos and shiny stones). Whole rooms were devoted to a boast: the limits of the known world assembled floor, walls, and ceiling, three dimensions covered in oddities chosen specifically to bathe an honored guest in wonder. At one time, collecting reptiles was a sign of good taste.

What is the attraction of camouflage greens; gnarled skins climbing and burrowing; and earthen smells; of life without warm blood and shapes that lack all connection to man? And yet these things draw a person to gardening. Reptiles are a kind of breathing garden. They have all the wonder and require all the same quiet care—plus, of course, some of them eat mice.

A snake-hunting friend of Ray Van Nostrand's refers to their passion as "the shine," after the boy in *The Shining* who had an extraworldly power he could not control. There may be no universal answer to why some people love what statistics suggest others readily drive a car over. Certainly there is the adventure of the chase, the chance to grab the only bit of nature that comes with a handle, an opportunity to interact with what is wild, to touch and to feel. Reptiles are vessels a keeper must pour himself or herself into if the keeper is to keep them alive. There are no plaintive meows, no puppy-dog eyes. A boy can keep one for a while believing he is taking good care of it.

It can be an addiction. Ray had gone through the reptile addict's progression—bigger, meaner, rarer, hot—so quickly he had skipped off the rails into a pirate's world. His penalty was federal prison. Prison is supposed to be a kind of reptile: ugly, frightening, dangerous.

Ray loved it. There were Friday night movies from five

to seven, games of eight ball, steaks for dinner. His family didn't visit so there was nothing to worry about. Phoenix was the kind of place rich people signed themselves into. He was feeling no withdrawal symptoms, he was losing some extra weight, and he was even catching kingsnakes in the prison yard. His fellow prisoners might not understand his passion, but they did understand his figures— there was money to be made in the reptile business.

His son Mike promised to keep it alive for him.

The Big Kid

The psychologist told Mr. and Mrs. Van Nostrand there was nothing they could do about their son. Michael had a control problem—not the usual child's lack of control, but an excess need to take control. If there was a vacuum, the specialist explained, young Mike would fill it.

He was a terrible child. He'd been born screaming and had never stopped. His mother didn't know where it came from. She wasn't like that. His father wasn't like that.

On the first day of elementary school, he ditched school and walked home. He punched Principal Hickey. He said "Fuck you" to his grade school teacher. Wherever Mike Van Nostrand went, he pulled behind him a furious dark cloud like a black balloon.

When Mike was a baby, his father would hold up a pipa pipa toad or a small turtle to show him, and he would try to eat it. He was eight years old the first time he remembers hunting snakes with his father. Mike made them a picnic—salami on Italian bread with mozzarella (which he pronounced "mootz," the way his father did, the New York way). They took the motorcycle and weren't gone long before his father cried out, "Look, Mike, there's two reds up there!"

In a flash, Ray strapped on his pole-climbing spikes and was rising up the tree trunk. When he got up to the snakes he found a hole with even more snakes inside.

"I'll throw them down to you and you put them in the bag!" he called.

One after another red rat snakes rained down from the tree; then came a seven-foot yellow rat snake. One after another Mike caught the snakes and wrangled them into a cloth snake bag. Every snake he caught bit him on the finger, every bite on the same spot. He was crying and bleeding when his father got down from the tree. "I don't want to catch snakes anymore," he told Ray.

But he did. He caught snakes many more times with his father, often riding on the hood of their red station wagon as they searched the back roads and sugarcane alleys. Sometimes his father would see a snake and hit the brakes in a way that landed Mike or his older brother, Ray Jr., right on top of their quarry. It wasn't bad being outside with your father.

Ray always brought a gun along. When things got dull they did some shooting. One time they saw a turkey buzzard passing overhead and his father aimed his .22 and shot it. What happened next created an image Mike would remember all his life. Instead of dropping out of the sky dead, the buzzard snaked its featherless head down to inspect its injury and, seeing food, pulled a beakful of its own guts and kept flying. It just kept flying away.

Visits to relatives in New Jersey included stops at good snake-hunting spots in the Pine Barrens. Everything seemed to somehow revolve around reptiles. Mike was still young the time he caught a large indigo snake eating a Florida garter snake. He knew he couldn't sell an indigo; they were protected. That right there was the difference between Mike and his father: Mike held on to the indigo, hoping it would let go of the garter snake so he could make some money. Ray collected so many indigos that there were times when their backyard seemed to bubble with an oil-blue pool. Eventually, their differences would emerge.

As Mike got older he helped with animal deliveries around Miami, including drops for Mario Tabraue's Zoological Imports. Business was so good that sometimes they could not drive across Miami without having to go back and restock the van.

By the time he was out of high school Mike knew he did not want to go into the reptile business. It wasn't the animals; it was the people. Since before he could walk they had come to his house, slinking around to the side door at the back of the garage. Sometimes the men brought their kids, and those kids would come into the house and play with Mike's toys. He did not like strange children playing with his toys. He did not like their fathers, either. They were degenerates, losers, middlemen who sold onward what his father caught or bought from locals or foreign exporters. Mike did not like it as a boy, and he did not like it later when he realized what else his father delivered with his van, and what else those men came for out there in his family's garage.

And so the boy who grew up the son of a leading reptile wholesaler did not go into the garage unless he had to, and he learned as little as possible about the reptile business. Still, as the son of Ray Van Nostrand he could not help learning something.

Mike was twenty-one years old, handsome in a Tom Cruise sort of way, and in his second year of accounting at Broward Community College, when word came down that his father was going to prison. Mike climbed into his Bronco. He wasn't a kid anymore. He was working nights at Delta Airlines. It wasn't anything much, just loading baggage, but it was his job, and his world, and he loved it. He had a serious girlfriend, too. They had met at Pet Fair, her father's pet shop. Her father and his father had known each other in New York, and Mike had worked for her father after graduating high school. Now they were dating. Michelle loved animals, but Mike couldn't wait to get away from them. The plan, if he had one, was that he would become a CPA and then maybe he and Michelle would get married.

He picked her up and together they drove to a local bar, where he knew the bartender and intended to put the friendship to good use. He and Michelle hardly talked about it on the drive. What was there to say? His father had beaten the government before, but that was with Mario Tabraue's help. This time the feds wanted Mario, and they were going to squeeze his father until they got him.

Operation Cobra, as it turned out, was a fitting name, given that the government was about to put Mike Van Nostrand in the reptile business.

After a couple of rounds of free drinks, Mike dropped Michelle off and drove home to see his father. Ray, as always, was out in the garage with his reptiles. He had partitioned off a section as a laundry area and then, from the floor to the ceiling, had built reptile cages and turtle tubs along the walls of the one-car garage.

Mike did not like animals. Once, in a shopping mall, he'd reached out to pet an old lady's dog and she had warned him, "Little boy, don't pet my dog, he bites." And so Mike had kicked her dog.

Now it seemed he had no choice. He badly wanted to be an accountant, but he had a five-year-old brother named Alex, and his mother, a high school teacher, was out of work. His father was leaving them with a triple mortgage. Mike stood with his father in the space they had used to pack tens of thousands of snakes, lizards, frogs, and turtles for shipment to pet shops and zoos around the globe.

He looked around at the cages.

"Do you think I can do this?" he asked.

Ray answered him in that sideways, never-look-them-in-the-eye way of his. "You can always make a decent living in the reptile business, Mike," he said. "Since I was a kid, I been in the fucking reptile business. Since I was eleven when I started going out and catching shit, selling it to the pet shops..."

The tricky part, Ray said, was not the animals; it was the people. "Bob will help you," Ray told him.

Mike knew Bob Udell as the man who used to pull up outside their house in the morning and yell, "Elaaaainnne—can Ray come out and plaaaayyyy?"

"Just keep your eye on him," Ray advised.

Mike dropped out of community college, took over his father's inventory, shouldered the responsibility of his mother and younger brother, and turned his old man's garage-based cocaine and reptiles business into a full-time reptile wholesale company.

"What are we going to call it?" his mother asked, the two of them sitting together at the kitchen table, the skeleton of reality lying open in the bank statements and bills spread between them.

"How about Strictly Reptiles," Mike said.

His mother smiled. Michael had always been a good storyteller; in two words he'd said it all.

He knew she liked it when he told her his stories. She would say, "That's good. Write that down." He tried, but the words that flowed so easily out of his mouth scurried away when he looked down at a piece of paper.

With his mother's help, Mike rented the end unit of a seedy little storefront a mile or two from their home. He packed up his father's cages and reptiles and moved them out of the house. Their new neighbors were a Joy gas station with heavily barred windows and a pawnshop that also sold guns. Strictly Reptiles' first location was barely the size of his family's one-car garage, but that did not matter. Mike could afford it—which is to say, he wanted those "customers" away from his family.

Ray did not like the idea of moving the business out of the house. He told Mike he would lose control. But there was not much his father could say; he was not allowed to conduct business over the telephone from federal prison.

And so it began.

Together Mike and Bob Udell would drive to the larger reptile dealers in South Florida, to Pet Farm and Ed Chapman's and Tommy Crutchfield's, where they'd cherry-pick iguanas and other low-cost species Mike could afford.

Mike was focused on volume. For years, that had meant supplying baby green turtles to be sold at department stores and on street corners across the United States. You could win a painted one at local carnivals, and you could buy paint sets to design their shells yourself. Unfortunately, you could also fit them in your mouth, which led to a lot of children getting salmonella poisoning. In 1975 the Food and Drug Administration had outlawed the sale of turtles less than four inches long, which had sent the baby green turtle market crashing down. Green iguanas were a ready alternative: only slightly more expensive and a bit harder to flush down the toilet, but still a little surprise to give your child. They were so popular, people were farming them by the millions in Central and South America for export to the United States. Almost every pet store in America that carried reptiles could be counted on to have green iguanas, which added up to a lot of green iguanas.

Mike's father turned out to be right about Bob Udell: he had a remarkable eye for choosing animals that could survive long enough to sell, but he also posed risks. First of all, he had been in the drug business. Second, he had worked for Philadelphia-based reptile smuggler Hank Molt. Third, he had left his most recent job, as manager at Martin's Aquarium, under a cloud. At Martin's, the stealing in the reptile section was so bad the owner not only had installed video cameras but also had mounted truck mirrors near his desk to keep an eye on the department. Udell had moved the truck mirrors and had taped pennies over the lenses on the video cameras.

Udell's cocaine habit was so bad that bloody clots would form inside his nose. He would pull these out and leave them on a windowsill to dry; when he was out of cocaine, he would eat his dried clots. He would do so many quaaludes he would ride up to a traffic light on his motor-cycle, forget to put his feet down, and fall over. He would go into a grocery store and eat an entire meal while walk-ing around shopping. Ray considered him the best thief he had ever seen, and a very knowledgeable reptile person.

Mike needed Udell. They built a room in the back of the shop so Udell could live there and watch over the ani-mals. Mike had to learn how to tell a good iguana from a bad one, and how to do it quickly, picking out a thousand at a time. Udell taught him that. After a few months, Udell said they should become partners. He had family money and said he needed $400 to go home and get it. When he got back, he said, he would buy into Strictly Reptiles and help Mike even more. Mike loaned him the money, but Udell did not come back. He never even left Florida. Mike discovered him living a few blocks away, and fired him. For a little while Udell tried to compete against Mike, but he was already lost. Udell left Florida, moved to Ohio, and within a year was found dead of an apparent drug overdose.

Ray criticized Mike for being too cautious with his money. He told Mike to buy first and pay later: Date the check two weeks out, he said, and make money selling.

But Mike did not want to do that. The men who came to deal with him were far more experienced than he was. Some helped him; some loaned him money or gave him favorable terms because of who his father was or because they knew his mother. But not everyone in the reptile business was looking out for his welfare, and even good men had their limits. The Van Nostrands lost their house.

Mike rented a smaller place. He watched out for his mother, and he cared for his little brother as if he were a son. He learned, too. Despite all his years around the animal world, he'd never known the ins and outs of importing and of paperwork, of getting an edge by skirting the rules.

He was buying a lot of his common green iguanas from a Miami dealer who was importing them from Suriname. The dealer had people bring iguanas and boa constrictors to Miami packed into suitcases with the proper paperwork. If customs asked if they had any wildlife, they would show them their paperwork; but if customs did not ask, then they would keep the paperwork and send it back down so someone else could bring up another suitcase. Iguanas were worth eight to ten dollars apiece back then, and men would transport hundreds of them in a single suitcase. They called it suitcasing, and for some it was a way of smuggling reptiles. For Mike, the would-be accountant, it was a game of shuffling paper, and he loved it.

Meanwhile, Ray had found his time locked up with mob hit men, Hell's Angels, and Mexican mafiosi rehabilitating. After serving eighteen months in prison, he got out, and Mike gave him a job. Ray said, All right, this is what we're gonna do. We're gonna hit everybody and we're gonna be first. And they did, and they were. If you were bringing a shipment in, Strictly Reptiles was the first one down to see you. Even if the Van Nostrands didn't have the money, Ray would write you a check and tell you to hold it for a week, and then they would sell it all.

The first year after Ray got out, Mike and his father did a million dollars in sales. That was the beginning. They moved out of the shop next to the Joy gas station and into another small building up the road a mile or two, off the Davie Road Extension. They quietly took control of Pet Farm's reptile division. For a multimillion-dollar operation, Strictly Reptiles was deceptively small, little bigger than a storefront. Its neighbor was a convenience store where men from the neighborhood openly sold crack and other drugs. Behind the building was a HUD development. Mike called it Niggertown.

Mike was now president and sole owner of one of the largest reptile import-export companies in the United States. His older brother, Ray Jr., a commercial fisherman with even less interest in reptiles than Mike, came ashore to join the family success. Elaine had left Ray while he was in prison. She was dating a man with wider interests—in travel, and wine, and books. When Mike found out, he went to the man's home at night and slashed his tires. He called the man awful names. But success was pouring into Strictly Reptiles so rapidly that before long Mike's anger washed past, and he gave his mother's boyfriend a job, too. They added a subtitle to their company name. They called themselves "The Iguana Kings."

Not even twenty-five years old, Mike Van Nostrand was pocketing over $200,000 a year, much of it cash. He had no real passion for animals. Collecting snakes, like his father did, out in the swamps and the sugarcane? You had to be crazy to like that. All he wanted to do, at heart, was have fun and drink beer with his old high school friends, but he rarely had time. He began biting his fingernails. Anything he could not control became an adversary, including food. In restaurants, he would order rapid-fire, as if his menu was some kind of scorecard. Just under six feet tall, his weight was expanding as fast as his business. His nose began to bleed because of his blood pressure.

He and Michelle married. They held their wedding at the only place suitable for two pet-shop kids in South Florida: Parrot Jungle. They moved into a place in the same community where he'd grown up. His business was close; his parents were both right around the corner, too. If they wanted to have kids, the new Brian Piccolo Park was almost across the street.

He was selling 200,000 to 300,000 green iguanas a year, half of the estimated U.S. total of the most popular imported reptile in the pet business. He was king of the bread-and-butter reptile trade. Nothing stayed in the shop for more than a week. They got it in, they got it out. If they couldn't sell it in a week they slashed the price and shipped it up to New York, including to Alfred Ojeda, the boy from the Bronx who now had his own reptile business.

Mike's father was right: birds were fashionable, birds were unfashionable; monkeys were popular, monkeys were unpopular. But reptiles never went out of style. They were never the flashiest item in the pet store, but they were almost always there—in a dish next to the cash register, or in the back, behind the cat litter and the hamsters. You could not go wrong in the reptile business.

And then, just as his father had before him, Mike saw a way to get a true rush out of the reptile business. His way.

The Easy Case

By the time Medina laid his head down on the pillow in his jail cell, Mike Van Nostrand knew his smuggler had been arrested. So he was not surprised when, a few weeks later, a squad car pulled up outside his building.

Friday, he thought. Feds always show up on Fridays. This one was Good Friday and the eve of Passover. But he was wrong: it was just Florida Fish and Game. He recognized these two. Lieutenant John West and Officer Charles Dennis stepped out of their car dressed in their Class B uniforms: dark green wool trousers and gray wool shirts, basketweave leather belts loaded with cop gear, and black Wellington boots.

"Hi, Mike," West said.

"Hi, John," Van Nostrand said.

West and Van Nostrand were friendly in the way executives and their IRS auditors often are. The state of Florida has a fairly generous view regarding wildlife kept within its borders. People keep an amazing array of exotic pets in Florida—tigers, lions, orangutans, parrots, large pythons, corals, tropical fish— and the business of selling those animals is big Florida business. The state is also the winter haven to Ringling Brothers and a host of other circuses, not to mention the home for Sea World, Monkey Jungle, Parrot Jungle, and, of course, Disney World.

In that way, the state of Florida and Michael Van Nostrand thought very much alike: exotic wildlife was a commodity, to be taxed in the case of the government and sold in the case of Strictly Reptiles.

Van Nostrand looked over West's shoulder. "Who's in the car with you?" he asked.

West turned. Parked next to the jacked-up Ford F-250 monster truck Van Nostrand drove to work was West's pea-green Crown Victoria.

"Oh, that's why I'm here," West said. He nodded toward the figure in the backseat of his car. "I figure it's just easier because you know me. His name is Agent Chip Bepler, from Fish and Wildlife."

Bepler got out of the car. Van Nostrand studied the new agent. Bepler was tall and lean. Something about him seemed different from the guy he was replacing, different from Jennifer English, who'd always struck Mike as a little too brittle, a little too eager to get him, which of course made him taunt her more. Penis envy, he considered it. At 320 pounds, Van Nostrand was not a man who indulged subtleties, but he had a feeling for people.

Bepler said he had a few things he wanted to talk to Mike about. One of them was a man named Tomas Medina.

"We're gonna take a look around, Mike," West interjected, and the two Florida officers left to inspect Van Nostrand's inventory.

Van Nostrand turned back to Bepler. He had nothing to hide, he said. He admitted that his company had a relationship with Pet Farm, and he said he did sometimes buy reptiles from a man named Tomas Medina. In fact, he noted, Medina had stopped by just a few days earlier and told him he had been arrested at the Miami airport for reptile smuggling.

I couldn't believe it, he said, adding that Medina had always told him his reptiles were captive-bred in the United States, perfectly legal.

That didn't make sense. Bepler asked why Medina would confess a crime to Van Nostrand if Van Nostrand had nothing to do with it.

Probably because we owed him money, Mike replied. Maybe he thought he was going to need it for a lawyer.

Did you pay him? Bepler wanted to know.

Van Nostrand had already discussed with his father how to handle paying Medina. He owed Medina around $8,000. Usually he wrote a check to his manager, Dale Marantz, who cashed the check and paid Medina, but not this time. Van Nostrand had known that eventually Medina would come asking for it.

You don't fucking pay him, his father said. *He got caught. You pay him it's like you're paying him to smuggle for you. They'll use that in court.* Of course, stiffing Medina for eight grand wasn't going to keep his mouth shut.

"No, I didn't pay him. He told me he got caught with smuggled animals. My lawyer said that's like ill-gotten gains. You can't pay a person who smuggled."

Van Nostrand loved this. Medina had come to his place wearing a wire, asking for his money. He was sure of it. There was no other reason for Medina to drive up from Miami and say what he did. Money was supposed to go to Medina through Pet Farm. Out of the blue, first time ever, he drives all the way up here from Miami saying he was arrested and that he wants his money? Even better, if Medina was wearing a wire, then it was Bepler who'd sent him. Van Nostrand repeated one of his favorite sayings to himself: *I might have been born at night, but it wasn't last night.*

Bepler asked Van Nostrand if he had any invoices documenting his transactions.

Van Nostrand said he thought so. It would probably take him a few days to dig them up.

For Bepler, reading people was like rubbing your fingertips over Braille. It was all right there for you if you let yourself feel the language. What people did with their hands, how their eyes moved and their pupils dilated, how their nostrils flexed, the moistness of their skin.

Bepler and his best friend in college had had a game they played at bars where one would introduce himself to a stranger as, say, an alligator wrestler, and then the other would come in on the story with something even better. They would throw each other lies all night, trying to keep the big lie from touching the ground. It was not a malicious game, but it helped him understand his own tells, and helped him to read others'.

He watched Van Nostrand. Mike's eyes were chameleon green. He did not offer Bepler a good look at them. He moved, shuffled paperwork, talked to employees. He was not shifty. He was not nervous. He was polite, but beneath that politeness Bepler could sense an anger. He had been warned about Van Nostrand's temper; he was not prepared for his control. His tell was that he did not have a tell—he looked right at you, not too long, just right. He didn't waver, but he didn't overdo it either. If he was lying, he was good—excellent, really.

And Bepler knew he was lying. They shook hands, and joined by Officers West and Dennis, Bepler prepared to go.

"Let me ask you something," Van Nostrand said. "Am I under investigation? Because if I am I think you have to tell me."

Inside, Bepler smiled. He liked this guy. He pushed back. Bepler was ten years older, and from what he knew there was a world of difference in how they'd grown up, but already they had something in common. With Medina's black book and Van Nostrand's invoices, it shouldn't be too hard to turn the easy case into a nice, fat conviction to start off his tenure in Miami.

"No," Bepler replied. "You're not under formal investigation. But I can't say I won't be back."

As the wildlife officers drove off in their car, Van Nostrand smiled. Bepler had made a huge mistake. The thing to do when you caught a smuggler coming into the country was to mark his animals, let the mule go, and follow him. It was called a "controlled delivery," and it was pretty basic stuff.

The only way Fish and Wildlife was ever going to catch him was if they got him red-handed. Even then, the government had to show he *knew* a law had been broken, which was almost impossible given the safeguards he took.

Van Nostrand turned back to his work. March was ball python season, so money was coming in. He imported thirty or forty thousand ball pythons from Togo each season.

The only other thing he cared about in the spring was baseball. Miami was on its way to getting its own major league team, the Florida Marlins. Van Nostrand didn't know Bepler's past or where he'd come from, but somebody should have told the guy he was in the big leagues now. First time up to the plate and Bepler had swung for the fence, like a rookie.

"That's the government for you," he said to himself. "Always in it for the short term."

~~~~~~

"Test me," Chip used to say to his sister, handing her a deck of flash cards with pictures of fish on one side and their names printed on the other. *Perch... pickerel...tarpon...gar...*

None of the family loved fishing the way Chip and his father did. The Bepler family creed, passed down from Grandpa Bepler, was simple: Catch and release. The rule was so rooted in the family that Chip's father could—and *would,* as Chip well knew—recount the two times they'd broken it: the two striped bass he and Chip caught at four A.M. off Cape Cod and ate with lobster for a real Down East dinner; and the trip they took with a guide off North Carolina's Currituck Sound, keeping one bass for their supper.

They'd traveled to Florida once, to Boca Grande, where

the big bay rushes in and out and the tarpon run with it. There were three of them: his grandfather, Charles Irving; his father, Dr. Charles Robert; and ten-year-old Chip, whose full name was Charles Robert Bepler Jr. They rented a boat, and for three nights and four days the Bepler men fished. They ran upriver into the Everglades during the day and came out into the bay at night to escape the mosquitoes. Chip's grandfather was a small man, a West Virginia mining executive, five foot four and 150 pounds. He hooked a tarpon bigger than he was and at that moment, right in front of Chip's eyes, the old man became a boy. Grandpa Bepler went home to West Virginia in tears. "This was one of the best trips I ever had," he said.

The Beplers lived on ten acres in Media, Pennsylvania, a small colonial town just southwest of Philadelphia. There was a spring on their property that years before had been a center of life for the Leni-Lenape Indians. At the foot of their property was a small pond, not much larger than a hockey rink. Geese and mallard ducks waddled up from Ridley Creek with their young to swim in the pond. Wood ducks built their nests in nearby trees. Deer drank from the water; so did foxes and pheasants. The Bepler children swam in the pond until the day their mother saw snakes crawling along the bank; then, at her insistence, a swimming pool was built close to the house. There were places nearby for Chip to fish, and often he would bring his catch home in a bucket, alive, and release what he'd caught into Bepler Pond. When older boys found out and tried to fish the pond, Chip and Dr. Bepler would chase them off, calling them "poachers."

On an occasion that would mark his future, young Chip released trout he'd caught into the pond. Trout are cold-water fish, and several of them died. A spring flowed separately from the pond, so Chip and his father damned the water flowing from the spring, squeezing it into a series of little pools, into which Chip released a few trout. The trout thrived for a while in the cold water, until raccoons discovered the wonderfully convenient cold-water fishbowls and ate the fish. Chip asked his father if they could use the swimming pool instead.

They pumped the chlorinated water out of the family swimming pool and pumped in the cool spring water. In the mornings Chip would carry bread to the swimming pool and scatter it across the water in a little-boy-sized half moon. In the winter, when the swimming pool froze, he crawled out along the diving board on his belly and broke a hole in the ice with a stick. Trout boiled up and took bread from his small hands. When spring came he scooped up the trout and returned them to Ridley Creek.

When the pond froze Chip learned to skate, and then to play hockey. He became captain of his high school team, but he was no all-American. He used his elbows. All six foot four of him would plunge into a corner, there'd be a tangle of pads and sticks and clashing plastic, and he would come out with the puck. When it was time for college, Dr. Bepler expected his son to go somewhere north, where it was cold and he could skate, since hockey had been the fabric of his high school years in Pennsylvania. Dr. Bepler had started at Princeton before switching to an accelerated medical school program established to meet the demands of the Korean War. Chip's older sister would go to Bryn Mawr on her way to a PhD in chemistry; his younger sister would get an MBA, as would his brother Tim. His brother Jonathan would get his master's in music.

Chip loved the ice, but his blood ran in and out with memories of that fishing trip he had taken to Florida with his grandfather. He went to college at the University of Tampa, studying marine biology. Upon graduation, he drove out to California and took a job at a water treatment plant. It was not a bright beginning for a marine biologist, but a career was not something he thought much about. A college pal, Dan Burleson, came out to stay with him and, growing tired of sleeping on Bepler's floor, found them both jobs as "biological technicians" with the National Marine Fisheries Service, part of NOAA, the National Oceanic and Atmospheric Administration, monitoring tuna boats for dolphin catch.

Like cowboys herding cattle, tuna fishermen in the Eastern Tropical Pacific—the triangle between San Diego, Hawaii, and Peru—used speedboats and great, quarter-mile-long purse seines to encircle dolphins and capture the tuna swimming below them. Bepler had an auditor's job, sitting on the deck with a pad, noting down how many dolphins his vessel had killed while hauling in tuna. NOAA forbade its monitors from either helping the fishing crew in their work or impeding them.

Bepler was required to watch while his ship corralled schools of tuna and then, according to a technique called the "back down" method, reversed direction, pulling one end of the net a little lower into the water so the captured dolphins could jump out. Bepler noticed that in their sleeping state, dolphins would sometimes drift to the bottom of the nets and drown. He put on his wet suit. He dove into the nets. He pushed out the dolphins. He stacked tuna, he played cards with the young male crew, he drank beer and told jokes. At the end of the season the boat's captain offered to hire him on as first mate, but Bepler had other plans.

It was his friend Burleson who came up with the idea of working for the U.S. Fish and Wildlife Service. It wasn't an idea really; it was more of an escape plan. Whenever they were about to go out on another tuna boat, they filed papers requesting any new job that would get them off months at sea with a pencil, talking about high school, and killing fish. Fish and Wildlife had openings for wildlife inspectors. Burleson took one in Texas, and Bepler went to Kennedy Airport in New York.

New York was one of the country's three largest ports, along with Los Angeles and Miami. All three saw a cross section of the world's wildlife, but there were differences. Los Angeles took in a good deal of Asian-sourced plants and animals. Miami was a dominant port for South American species. New York was the key port for America's fashion industry—designers and manufacturers employing almost every nonedible part of an animal: skins, furs, feathers, various kinds of wool, bones, teeth, shells.

Bepler's job was to check shipping documents. The major international treaty covering trade in wildlife, CITES (the Convention on International Trade in Endangered Species of Wild Fauna and Flora), required that endangered wildlife and wildlife products travel with export paperwork from their source country; in cases of the most endangered animals, import authorization from the destination country was also required. It was a good system, but it had some enormous holes. You could spend a lifetime staring at paperwork.

Instead, Bepler popped open shipping crates. He liked putting his hands on a shipment, and he liked the challenge of distinguishing legal products from illegal ones. Fashion houses sometimes tried importing one species of crocodile leather labeled as another, for example; boutiques would try to sneak in shahtoosh, the prized Tibetan antelope wool so fine an entire shawl could be pulled through a wedding ring.

Of all the tricksters he saw, he found the live-reptile smugglers to be the most ingenious. Reptiles were hardy and flexible, and because they were cold-blooded you could lower their body temperatures and they would not move. Smugglers taped the legs of tortoises and balled them into sweat socks. They hid snakes in false crate bottoms and in secret compartments in their luggage. Importers tested your knowledge, counting on you not to know whether fifty dirt-covered baby tortoises were all Indian star tortoises, Burmese star tortoises, or—a crown jewel in the smugglers' world—Madagascan plowshare tortoises.

Looking inside crates was a lot more fun than poring over paperwork. Plus, with reptiles you could pick them up. He was a wildlife officer, after all.

He bought an old wooden boat, like Quint's in *Jaws* and about as reliable, docked it in Reynolds Channel, off Long Beach, Long Island, and made it his home. He took his showers at the YMCA. He met a wildlife inspector named Robin Tannen and fell in love.

After he and Bepler had been wildlife inspectors for four years, Dan Burleson called with the news that Fish and Wildlife's Division of Law Enforcement had openings for special agents. Instead of watching it come in all day, like bookkeepers on Noah's Ark, they could be criminal investigators. "Why don't we do it?" Burleson suggested.

Bepler hopped into his rusted white Dodge pickup truck and drove down to Glynco, Georgia, to start classes at FLETC, the Federal Law Enforcement Training Center. FLETC was serious business to Fish and Wildlife headquarters. It was the training school for the Secret Service, the ATF, the IRS, and other federal law enforcement agencies that lacked in-house facilities like those at the CIA or the FBI. If you did not pass FLETC, you did not become a special agent—*and* you had no guarantee that you could return to your inspector's job.

The first half of the course was Criminal Investigator School; the second half was Special Agent Basic School. FLETC was a boot camp for criminal law and procedure, international and domestic environmental law, investigative techniques, and wildlife identification. Burleson and Bepler rented a town house together and made a pact: no beer drinking the night before an exam. Fifteen weeks later Chief Clark R. Bavin handed them their gold badges. They were special agents, empowered to carry a gun and make arrests. Bepler was given a stainless-steel Smith & Wesson model 66, a .38.

Burleson moved to Missouri. Bepler went back to New York, one of the worst posts in the country for any federal law enforcement officer because of the cost of living; it was worse still for anyone interested in the outdoors. There was virtually no wildlife in New York City, but Robin was there.

In the summer of 1988, Ray Van Nostrand was just settling into prison life in Phoenix, Mike Van Nostrand was setting up his first reptile shop, and rookie Special Agent Chip Bepler was looking for a way to make a difference.

Bepler asked his new supervisor, Special Agent Saverio "Sam" LiBrandi, what he should focus on. LiBrandi raised his eyebrows. They had only three special agents in the office. Duck season they did duck hunters. Deer season they did deer hunters. Following up seizures by wildlife inspectors at Kennedy International alone could fill an agent's day. LiBrandi kept that to himself. Unofficially, he was Bepler's mentor as well as his boss, and he knew it was especially important to foster a new agent's enthusiasm.

"Well, Chip," LiBrandi said, "you were an inspector. How about live reptiles?"

Bepler picked up a copy of *Newsday,* a local paper, and turned to the classifieds, scanning for people selling reptiles. He did the same with other periodicals, and when he found something that looked like it might be more than a teenager with a boa constrictor to get rid of he called the seller and introduced himself. If it sounded promising, then after work or on the weekend he drove to the guy's house.

LiBrandi watched, fascinated. LiBrandi had never done any significant undercover work. There was no need to, and for reasons he was not yet ready to disclose, there was no point. Certainly he'd never dreamed that reptiles were such a gateway to wildlife crime. It seemed like every little dinky classified ad Bepler answered led to something protected, some salamander or frog or bog turtle that was illegal to collect or sell. The owners either had something in their home or they knew somebody who was into something that was a state or federal wildlife violation.

With his boss's encouragement, Bepler opened up an undercover case in cooperation with the New York State Department of Environmental Conservation.

To fund it, LiBrandi got Bepler permission to sell their civil case seizures—boa constrictors and other pet-shop fare imported in violation of minor rules—and Bepler kept going, trading and selling, and getting back more and more protected wildlife. He started to learn the names of dealers in New York and around the country. He began seeing patterns in where animals came from and where they went. In one case, his office caught a guy smuggling alligators across the border to Canada. The man's supplier was a company in Florida called Strictly Reptiles. Bepler heard the name Mike Van Nostrand mentioned with increasing frequency.

Reptile collectors were unlike buyers of any other form of wildlife he had ever seen. They had to have it. One agent friend of Bepler's joked that the addiction was so strong he was surprised no defense counsel had proposed a boa constrictor version of the "Twinkie Defense." Bepler did not have any special love for reptiles. They meant no more to him than any other kind of wildlife. In fact, he probably cared less about them. He really didn't understand the obsession he saw in reptile collectors. What meant a great deal to him was the illegal exploitation of wildlife on a commercial scale. *That* he hated.

It had been going on for more than a century: the mass killing of the passenger pigeon by restaurant-supplying "market hunters"; the shooting of the bison by professionals working for the army, the railroads, or the skin or tongue trades; the destruction of the famous Cuthbert Lake rookery, the Everglades' home to egrets and herons, shot out in 1904 by the plume industry to make women's hats.

The Fish and Wildlife Service was not like other federal law enforcement agencies, which had villains like John Dillinger or Al Capone to color their history. The great auk, the Carolina parakeet, the eastern elk—the history of Bepler's profession was recorded in victims. He could not do much against habitat destruction, pollution, or any of the other amorphous problems facing wildlife, but he could do something about commercial profiteers.

He drove out to see New York–area reptile dealers, and he made his cases. If he could find their main engine, he would stop it.

Bepler was having so much success, and so much fun, Sam LiBrandi felt sorry about finally having to break the bad news to him.

"Chip," he said one day, "you know we're not going to be able to prosecute any of these guys, right?"

Bepler stared at his boss.

U.S. Fish and Wildlife cannot get a criminal case through the U.S. Attorney's Office, LiBrandi told Bepler. The reason was simple. Their cases were prosecuted by the U.S. Attorney's Office in Brooklyn, home to John Gotti. Gotti was currently public enemy number one, and he was not the only problem for the Brooklyn office. The Lucchese and Gambino crime families had turned Kennedy International Airport into a candy store. Half the prosecutor's resources were allocated to fighting interstate and international drug trafficking. Complaints were coming into the U.S. Attorney's Office about its failure to attack public corruption and financial crimes. There was no room in a prosecutor's day for a Pine Barrens tree frog. All Bepler could do, LiBrandi explained, was give anyone he caught dealing reptiles a civil fine.

Bepler understood the argument, but he disagreed with LiBrandi's conclusion. He wasn't going to give a guy a hundred-dollar ticket and lose an asset. If they couldn't prosecute, he was going to develop the guy, and see if he led to somebody bigger. LiBrandi's fascination increased. Bepler had such a good personality, he was soon turning violators into informants right and left. For years, a lack of prosecutorial support had left agents in New York feeling beleaguered. Now, Bepler was taking a flaw in the system and turning it to their advantage: Bepler was building an intelligence operation.

Finally, the day came when he did have a case large enough to take to the U.S. Attorney's Office. A man had sold him an illegal American alligator, which Bepler had ignored. Then the man had offered Bepler a barn owl. Selling a barn owl was a Migratory Bird Treaty Act violation, a flat-out felony.

"What do you think, Sam?" Bepler asked.

LiBrandi agreed. As U.S. Fish and Wildlife special agents they couldn't walk away from a felony; anyway, it was a barn owl, not a reptile—the federal prosecutor *had* to take a barn owl.

Bepler knocked on the man's door wearing a wire. Once inside, he identified the barn owl, gave the signal, and LiBrandi and other agents rushed the house. To preserve Bepler's cover, they arrested him, too. Afterward, a proud LiBrandi sat close enough to eavesdrop while Bepler telephoned the prosecutor's office and shared their good news.

"You did *what*?" the prosecutor asked. "You arrested a guy for selling you *an owl*?!"

"Well, it's a felony," Bepler said.

He took the phone away from his ear. The prosecutor was screaming. They laughed about it later—"They're trying to make a RICO case on Gotti and we're calling about alligators and barn owls!"—but laughing didn't salve the sting.

After three years of gathering intelligence, Bepler understood where he needed to be: the biggest fish in reptile smuggling were all in South Florida. One of those fish was growing much faster than the others. Bepler had no reason to think he would have any more success prosecuting Mike Van Nostrand than he'd had prosecuting his barn owl poacher, but on that point, at least, luck was with him.

Law of the Jungle

Chris McAliley joined the U.S. Attorney's Office in Miami to try cases. She got cases agents made on the street—"reactive cases" they called them. Drug buys generally, firearms cases, cases involving the smuggling of aliens. Usually simple and usually small.

Part of the job was traveling down to Key West occasionally to act as prosecutor at the federal courthouse there. This was a roaming "calendar" duty reminiscent of the circuit judge's life. Her second year as a prosecutor, McAliley and another assistant U.S. attorney were tapped for a two-week calendar of "boat cases"—drugs on go-fast boats, drugs on Panamanian tankers, drugs on sloops. The vessels and the hiding places varied, but the crimes were the same, and popular. While she was there she met the National Marine Fisheries Service agent assigned to Key West. His name was Dan O'Brien, and he was upset with her office. "We can't get anyone to take our cases," he told her.

He was referring to sea turtle cases—fishing for them, taking the eggs. "They're all federal crimes," he said.

McAliley had never heard of a sea turtle case. "You get somebody who killed a turtle," she told him, "and I'll take the case."

She was surprised by how soon O'Brien knocked on her door. He'd brought photographs. The suspect's name was Raymond Martinez. He lived with his girlfriend in a stilt home on Sugarloaf Key. Martinez had gone out fishing and come home with a 250-pound live loggerhead turtle. An anonymous caller had tipped off the Florida Marine Patrol, saying that two people were under their deck butchering a sea turtle with a knife and an axe.

McAliley examined the photographs. It looked like a murder. There was blood on the gaff, blood in the boat, and a cut-up turtle.

When the marine police had driven up, Martinez had fled in a Camaro, tossing turtle parts from the car like a dealer jettisoning drugs. A sea turtle case might be new to McAliley, but it looked as if Martinez knew he was doing something wrong. During their search, agents had found flippers from an endangered hawksbill turtle in the suspect's freezer.

McAliley took the case, and Martinez got six months in jail for killing a threatened loggerhead turtle, the maximum sentence under the Endangered Species Act. Both the *Miami Herald* and the *Miami News* covered the story favorably.

Still, McAliley was uncertain about how people in Key West would react to her prosecuting a local for sea turtle poaching. They were an independent group down there. They called themselves "Conchs" and jokingly threatened to secede from the rest of the country as the "Conch Republic." Jokes aside, there were a lot of people in Key West who had gone to the edge of America to escape the law, not to support it.

She was in a taxi, riding to the Key West airport, when the subject came up with her cabdriver. "Oh, the Martinez case," the driver said. "The guy who killed the loggerhead and got six months!" The cabdriver recited the whole case for her. He was surprised by the prison time, he said, but he thought the guy deserved it.

The case had made a positive impact.

The week after Martinez's conviction, the *Key West Citizen* published an editorial reminding locals that the Tortugas had gotten their name because of how plentiful turtles had been when Columbus arrived. The paper not only supported McAliley's federal prosecution, but also used her case to point out that Florida's state penalty for killing a sea turtle was no heavier than its penalty for stealing bubble gum. There had been two hundred loggerhead turtles nesting in Key West, the editorial said. The week Martinez pled guilty a second person was found with a dead sea turtle. The title of the piece was "Now There Are 198."

McAliley began reading about sea turtles. Five of the world's seven species could be found in Florida waters. All of them were protected by the Endangered Species Act.

This was something worth pursuing.

The following summer police found James E. "Prince of the Beach" Bivens covered in sand, walking along the road on Jupiter Island carrying a sack. Jupiter Island was one of the country's most exclusive beach communities, future home to singer Celine Dion and golfers Greg Norman and Tiger Woods: carrying a sack at night was not normal behavior. Bivens had on him 818 turtle eggs, including not only "threatened" loggerhead turtle eggs but also green turtle eggs. Green turtles were an endangered species. Nearby, the beach showed drag marks leading from plundered nest to plundered nest. A month earlier, state officers had caught Bivens stealing 1,088 turtle eggs. He was peddling the eggs at bars and on street corners as an aphrodisiac. They were a buck or two each, and you chased them down with a beer. Mexican restaurants sold them, and Old Floridians believed that a cake baked with sea turtle eggs would hold moisture longer than one made with chicken eggs.

McAliley prosecuted Bivens, who faced more time than Martinez because of the green turtle. She made history, said the *Miami Herald,* after Bivens was sentenced to two years in prison and three years of probation, again reportedly the stiffest sentence ever handed out under the Endangered Species Act.

Her colleagues gave McAliley a nickname. They called her the turtle prosecutor.

McAliley telephoned headquarters and asked for John T. Webb, assistant chief for the Wildlife and Marine Resources Section, the Justice Department's leading attorney on wildlife crime. "Tell me about Lacey," she said. "Tell me about CITES."

The Lacey Act was the country's oldest national wildlife statute. Originally drafted in 1900 to stem domestic waterfowl and game poaching, the amended Lacey Act made it a federal crime to import or export wildlife in violation of any state, federal, Indian, or *foreign* law. The last condition was remarkable. Many countries have laws on their books they either cannot or will not enforce. In some cases, wildlife smugglers bribe foreign officials to ignore their law. Under the Lacey Act, it was a federal crime to violate another country's wildlife laws. If China said what you did to a butterfly in its territory was illegal and you brought that butterfly into Miami, the United States could prosecute you, and the penalties you faced were not China's, they were America's—and they were felonies.

McAliley had never heard of a law with such an international reach. The Lacey Act made the United States the world's environmental watchdog. But that was true only on paper. Prosecutors with the will and resources to take Lacey Act cases were rare. These cases could be terribly demanding—they required learning foreign law, locating foreign witnesses and shipping records, and sometimes, seeking extradition of smugglers. Even with the help of headquarters in Washington, D.C., Lacey Act cases were still too much for most federal prosecutors, whose plates were already piled high with typical human crimes.

For McAliley, it was fascinating. One minute she was prosecuting a run-of-the-mill marijuana case, the next minute she was back at her desk, reading Senegalese rules on African gray parrots, feeling the globe expand with the chance to do some real good. CITES was an international trade agreement for wildlife. It classified the natural world into two main "appendices" agreed on by the parties involved. Appendix I species were threatened with extinction (for example, eastern lowland gorillas, tigers, Asiatic elephants), and their commercial trade was forbidden. Appendix II species were considered potentially vulnerable but still abundant enough that their *regulated* commercial trade was allowed. A good many of the wild animals in international trade are Appendix II species—boa constrictors and green pet-shop iguanas, for example. The goal of CITES was to stop commercial flows of Appendix I species and, through a permit and quota system, to moderate the commercial flow of Appendix II species. A third appendix listed species of concern to an individual country and required authorization from the listing country to be traded. Exceptions existed, and one important exception allowed unlimited commercial trade of Appendix II animals born in captivity. McAliley was not particularly interested in captive-bred animals. Her concern was poaching.

Under CITES each country policed itself, and to some extent that was where the Lacey Act came in. If a country did not enforce its own laws, the United States could enforce those laws for it, at least when it came to wildlife entering the United States.

McAliley saw real merit to the cases she was prosecuting, and she considered them an important way to give life to a new era she saw developing in U.S. law. The daughter of famed labor lawyer Thomas McAliley, she'd still been a girl growing up in Florida when Congress began enacting laws at the heart of environmental protection: the Clean Air Act, the Clean Water Act, the Endangered Species Act, the Superfund statute, and others. Those laws were proof that the country cared deeply about what was happening to its environment.

She had graduated from NYU Law School as a prestigious Root-Tilden scholar for public service; she had clerked for a federal judge; and she'd just been starting out as a federal prosecutor when Congress began to bolster those environmental laws with new teeth. In 1987 Congress increased penalties in the Clean Water Act. It did the same in 1990 for Clean Air. McAliley believed prosecutors should operate within the framework of laws they are given. It was one thing for people to talk about the environment; it was another for Congress to take action. Increasing criminal penalties meant federal prosecutors should take pollution and wildlife cases more seriously.

McAliley thought about the wildlife cases she had seen. These people acted like genuine criminals. They were smuggling, creating false documents, laundering funds, victimizing the public, *and* hurting wildlife. The profile of a wildlife smuggler exactly matched the profile of a drug smuggler; plus, there was an added victim: the animal itself.

She began looking into the type of wildlife coming into the United States, the source countries, and the patterns. The species and routes varied but not the destination. Miami was *driving* illegal takings around the world.

South Florida was home to some of the country's rarest and most diverse ecosystems. Extending from Key West to Indian River, the southern half of the state alone encompassed Lake Okeechobee, the Everglades, the Gulf Stream current, and coral reefs; the entire state was a national environmental treasure. And yet there was not one federal prosecutor in Florida with institutional knowledge of environmental law.

Even worse, when it came to deciding which offenses to prosecute in the Miami office, wildlife cases went to the catchall "major crimes" section, where they competed for resources against drug and gun cases. It was a very plain reality: a smuggled parrot had no chance against a drug-filled Panamanian tanker. It was the same Gotti-versus-a-barn-owl problem Bepler and LiBrandi had seen in New York. *Chip, you know we're not going to be able to prosecute any of these guys, right?* Miami was so overwhelmed on drugs that the prosecutorial guideline for taking on marijuana cases was "nothing under 100 kilos."

Who could take on a turtle egg case?

McAliley looked in the mirror. She had just won a major case against the U.S. Sugar Corporation for dumping hazardous waste near Lake Okeechobee. The penalty—$3.75 million—had been celebrated as the largest criminal fine ever imposed under the hazardous waste law. She had a reputation for obtaining harsh penalties. If she was going to do it, now was the time.

She went to her boss, U.S. Attorney Dexter Lehtinen, with a proposal to create an environmental crimes section. The section would stand on its own, equal to major crimes, narcotics, public corruption, and other sections in the Miami prosecutor's office. It would be a mini version of two sections found only at Justice Department headquarters: the Environmental Crimes Section, which focused on pollution, and the Wildlife and Marine Resources Section, which focused on wildlife trafficking. Her section would go after both. As far as she knew, no other U.S. attorney's office in the country had one.

Lehtinen was a man with an aggressive reputation. He was ex-army and had had part of his face blown off in Laos. More recently, without informing his superiors at the Justice Department, he had sued the state of Florida over pollution in the Everglades. His motto was "No guts, no glory."

Lehtinen gave her a green light, and in 1992 McAliley established the Environmental Crimes Section in Miami. For the first time in history, the U.S. Fish and Wildlife Service, the Environmental Protection Agency, and other federal law enforcement agents would not have to compete against other types of criminal cases to prosecute environmental crimes in South Florida.

McAliley had a philosophy for her new section. Their resources were limited, and they would not be able to take down everybody. They would choose their targets. The question she wanted her team members to ask themselves was, Do people in the industry know the defendant, and would they be affected by his or her imprisonment?

McAliley and Bepler became quick friends. They took their families camping together. Still, Bepler did not discuss his cases much. Even at home, at family gatherings, Robin would say, "Chip, tell your brother about the piping plover" or another case. Sometimes Chip would tell that story, but often he would try to find a story that wasn't connected to what he was working on. More and more he was discovering that reptile hobbyists were in more places than one might expect. More and more he was coming to believe that there was something important at stake beyond green lizards. What it was, he didn't quite know yet. McAliley had the same feeling.

McAliley made it clear that if Bepler could get Mike Van Nostrand to her door, her Environmental Crimes team would prosecute him. Bepler was both astonished and grateful. For the first time a team of prosecutors had his back. History said he was going to need them.

The First Bullet

The godfather of American reptile smuggling started out of the same gun, as he liked to say, as Ray Van Nostrand. As boys they read the same books; they haunted the same zoo triangle—the Bronx Zoo, the Staten Island Zoo, and the Philadelphia Zoo; they belonged to the same herpetological societies. While Ray moved to Florida and followed a path into crimes unrelated to reptiles, Henry A. Molt Jr. stayed home, just outside of Philadelphia, cultivating an elite clientele. In later years, Molt would operate from behind a locked door. He would use a peephole to identify his visitors. His customers were the only ones in the country in the 1970s who could afford rare reptiles, and together they funded the most exclusive reptile smuggling operation America has ever known. Molt's customers were America's top zoos.

Molt was an adventurer. He modeled himself

after freelance big-game collectors like Frank Buck, whose books and movies about life in pursuit of giraffes, elephants, and hippopotamuses he had loved as a boy. (John Wayne's rhinoceros-chasing character in *Hatari!* was based on Buck.) Molt wore a tailored safari outfit made for him in Thailand. He'd gone to college. He quoted Shakespeare, enjoyed Mozart. Anticipating both Indiana Jones and his nemesis, Dr. Rene Belloq, he was highly intelligent, relentless, and got what his clients wanted.

In a single 1973 collecting trip, Molt traveled to Fiji, the Solomon Islands, Papua New Guinea, the Philippines, Hong Kong, Singapore, Thailand, and India, dodging government regulations, before returning home with reptiles for his clients. The National Zoo in Washington, D.C., got its shipments, as did the Dallas Zoo, the Sacramento Zoo, the Seneca Park Zoo, the St. Louis Zoo, the Philadelphia Zoo, and others. Molt supplied the zoo world with rare reptiles, and before he was through, he nearly destroyed them all.

Molt came from a well-to-do family. His father operated a plumbing and heating business and was councilman in the government of Jenkintown, Pennsylvania, a quaint village just north of Philadelphia.

As a boy Molt ran the local streams and woods, flipping rocks and logs, looking for any kind of reptile. He read voraciously and idolized the deans of American popular herpetology, especially those who wrote books about their adventures: Raymond L. Ditmars at the Bronx Zoo, Clifford H. Pope at the Field Museum, Carl Kauffeld at the Staten Island Zoo.

His hero was Ross Allen, founder of Ross Allen's Reptile Institute in Silver Springs, Florida, the famous venom-extraction center. During World War II alone, Allen's facility milked 73,960 venomous snakes, providing the raw material for antivenom bought by the U.S. military. Allen was one of the world's foremost experts on the American alligator; as if that were not enough, he was also a stand-in for Johnny Weissmuller in *Tarzan*. Allen folded his research into a tourist attraction, with alligator wrestling, snake milking, a Seminole Indian village, and a gift shop. He proved you could make a very good living at reptiles, once you found the right niche.

Molt lived a few minutes' north of the Philadelphia Zoo, "America's first zoo," where the famous herpetologist Roger Conant was curator. Conant's *A Field Guide to Reptiles and Amphibians of Eastern and Central North America* is the most popular work on reptiles ever written, the little blue book owned by every creek-stomping, lizard-chasing boy or girl in America (even on the West Coast). In Philadelphia, Conant was a celebrity. He had his own radio show, *Let's Visit the Zoo,* which began each week with a recorded lion's roar, a sound the entire city came to know. As a teenager, Molt wrote letters to Conant about his interest in reptiles, and Conant, much to the boy's delight, wrote him back.

With all his heart, Molt wanted to be a reptile keeper at the Philadelphia Zoo. After years of dreaming, he finally worked up the nerve and wrote Conant, asking him for a job. Conant turned him down flat. So did Molt's hero, Ross Allen. Molt wrote more letters, and got more rejections.

He took a job with Kraft Foods, and got married. His days were homogenized. He spent them in a suit and a tie, shelving mayonnaise at the Acme supermarket in South Philadelphia. The supermarket had been built on the grounds of Moyamensing Prison (where affable Herman Webster Mudgett, alias H. H. Holmes, the serial killer of the 1893 World's Fair, had been hanged). As far as Molt was concerned, it was still a prison site.

During a flight back from a sales meeting in Chicago, a stranger seated next to Molt started complaining about his job. He worked for IBM, he said, and had to wear a hat and a white shirt to work and was forced to do everything else Molt hated almost as much as he hated listening to a guy complain about his life.

The man finished and asked, "What do you do for a living?"

Molt lied to him: "I go around the world collecting reptiles for zoos."

The IBM man's eyes froze, and in them Molt saw his future. It had nothing to do with mayonnaise. He made some contacts, quit his job, and bought a pet shop. He cleared out the dogs and the fish and turned it into one of the world's first all-reptile shops.

He named his business Philadelphia Reptile Exchange. To fill it, he reached out to anyone and any place he could think of. He wrote to foreign universities and museums looking for reptiles and contacts. If he saw a Peruvian priest in *National Geographic,* he wrote to the man and developed a contact. From the beginning he went after only the rarest animals, the kind a zookeeper might want.

A major break came when he discovered a man in the Netherlands who could supply him with protected Australian animals. It turned out that the man's son was the director of the Melbourne Zoo, and he was also a reptile smuggler. William Van Aperen began smuggling reptiles directly to Molt, in packages labeled as china, glassware, or ceramics. A rich woman in Switzerland was interested in U.S. reptiles and supplied Molt with another steady source. Molt took his first collecting trip to Africa. On his own, he traveled to Nigeria, Ghana, South Africa, Mozambique, Madagascar, Uganda, Kenya, Egypt, and Germany in search of reptiles and contacts.

In 1965, Molt sat down at his father's typewriter and tapped out his first price list. The list took up only a single sheet of paper, but what he had accumulated was as impressive as the reptile house in any zoo. He mimeographed the price list and mailed it to eighteen or twenty zoos, including the ones that had rejected him. The twenty-five-year-old did not expect to get their business. He wrote to them, as he would recall years later, to say, *Fuck you! You wouldn't hire me—now look what I got!*

To his surprise, zoo curators did not write him back. They *phoned.* They wanted to buy.

As research institutions, zoos and museums could legally acquire most of the species they wanted, but that involved a lot of red tape. Somehow, Molt made the tape disappear. The zoo world did not know how, and they did not want to know. Hank Molt became their dark hand.

In the Philippines he bribed a zookeeper and had reptiles from the Manila Zoo brought to his hotel room. He carried a pair of baby saltwater crocodiles home to Philadelphia in his briefcase. When the Papua New Guinea government denied him permission to collect because he was a known commercial dealer, the Philadelphia Zoo arranged for a Molt straw man to act as the zoo's territorial representative, and Molt got the zoo its reptiles. To conceal his full travels, he carried more than one passport. He timed shipments to arrive in Philadelphia on Friday evenings, after the inspectors had gone home.

The zoos and museums loved what he brought them:

> *Dear Hank:*
> *. . . The New Guinea tree frogs arrived in good order. Thank you. They are beautiful creatures. I really dig them. . . .*
> > *J. S. Dobbs*
> > *Curator [Atlanta Zoo]*

They broadened his cover:

> *To Whom It May Concern:*
> *This will introduce Mr. Hank Molt, of the Philadelphia Reptile Exchange. Any courtesies that can be extended to aid him in his work would be very much appreciated. Thank you.*
> > *Sincerely,*
> > *Ray Pawley*
> > *Curator of Reptiles, Brookfield Zoo*

They even wanted his dead:

> *Dear Hank:*
> *. . . It occurred to me, too late to mention it to you in Philadelphia, that we might be able to make a mutually profitable arrangement. I am sure that you suffer*

*some loss of specimens. . . . We are building a collection
of skeletal material here. . . .*
    Yours Sincerely,
    Clarence J. McCoy, Jr. [Carnegie Museum]

    *P.S.: Could you please send me one of your mimeo-
graphed price lists?*

Finally, on April 1, 1968, Hank Molt got what he
wanted most of all:

Dear Mr. Molt
*. . . This letter is to inquire whether, in your expe-
rience, the crocodile market is still firm, or whether
conservation activities or the poaching for the
leather industry are making it difficult to obtain
specimens. . . . We will be in the market for many
things, and perhaps you might be able to help us obtain
them. May I suggest that you call me. . . .*
    Sincerely yours,
    Roger Conant [Philadelphia Zoo]

They did not want only reptiles. The assistant curator
of birds at the Bronx Zoo sent him a list of birds of paradise species to collect. The assistant director at Chicago's
Lincoln Park Zoo positively frothed for lemurs:

*Obviously we are very interested in any Lemurs
you might come up with while in Madagascar. At
present we need a female White-fronted, female Red-
fronted and a male Fat-tailed Dwarf Lemur, genus
Cheirogaleus. We also want Ruffed, either color phase,*

*as you already know, Black Lemurs and Crowned Lemurs which is a sub-species of Mongoose Lemur. If you come up with Gray Gentle Lemurs (*Hapalemur*) we'd be interested in those too.*

Zookeeping can be a surprisingly competitive profession. Caring for animals is expensive. To pay the bills, zoos need people coming through their gates. Some species attract more patrons than others. "Charismatic megafauna" like orangutans, elephants, and panda bears bring in revenue. Baby gorillas are cuter than mature gray-haired ones. A successful zoo knows how to manage its animal inventory, moving out the old and borrowing the unusual, to bring in customers.

Zoos also compete on a less public level, one that has nothing to do with money. It has to do with prestige. First to discover, most rare, most complete collection of a genus, longevity record, first to breed—zoo literature is rife with hints of the one-upsmanship among directors and curators. The public may have no clue about whether the iguana they're looking at is from Fiji or Florida, but a reptile curator knows, and so do his peers.

Until Molt, reptiles were not a priority with most zoos. Even though reptile houses have always been among the most popular destinations in a zoo, the species inside have rarely been given much priority. For years, reptile curators had to build their collections from the leavings of bird and mammal expeditions, often those out of South America. No one knew how to sex, let alone breed many common reptile species. Like their bird relatives, reptiles' sex organs are concealed inside the single excretory vent, the cloaca. It was not until 1967, for example, that

Peter Brazaitis at the Bronx Zoo stuck his index finger into a sleeping alligator's cloaca and discovered how to sex gators. You just had to try things. The simplest tricks made the biggest differences. The discovery that even jungle and desert species required a dark, cool period to get their sex hormones flowing opened the door to predictable breeding. Today elementary school children breed in classrooms what herpetologists as late as the 1970s considered impossible. In Molt's era, running a reptile house was like owning a flower shop: some species you expected to take root, but most you threw away, then ordered more.

Molt offered reptile curators a king's reach. By freelancing he bestowed on his customers the same rush that royalty for all of man's history has enjoyed: the charge from opening a crate sent home by an army on crusade, by a Christopher Columbus, or by a Dutch or British East India Company explorer.

His Indiana Jones–like talent for bringing home trophies offered reptile curators a chance for something their mammalian and avian colleagues had known for a century: respect. He focused on five zoos he considered especially competitive with one another when it came to reptiles: Houston, Dallas, Columbus, Fort Worth, and Cincinnati. As if training guard dogs, he sold to them in rationed bits, offering each one just enough treats to keep it aggressive.

~~~~~~

At three o'clock on a cold Tuesday afternoon, January 14, 1975, two United States customs agents entered the Philadelphia Reptile Exchange and asked to look at Molt's import records. Molt had brushed the agents off the previous week, telling them through a partially opened door that he had not imported any wildlife in over two years. This time the agents were more insistent, and Molt unlocked his filing cabinet.

What happened next changed history.

After studying Molt's financial records, and immersing themselves in the science and the business of reptiles, the two customs agents, Joseph O'Kane and John Friedrich, accompanied by Assistant U.S. Attorney Thomas E. Mellon Jr., boarded an airplane and conducted a forty-five-day around-the-world investigation, retracing Molt's international smuggling operation country by country, village by village.

Newswires across America lit up with what they discovered. "Washington's Zoo Accused of Purchasing 'Hot' Lizards," exclaimed the *Washington Star*. "A Slimy Smuggling Business," said the *Philadelphia Inquirer*, "Rare Reptiles 'more profitable than heroin.'"

The *Washington Post* reported:

A federal investigation into snake smuggling, involving hundreds of thousands of dollars' worth of rare reptiles and some of the nation's leading zoos, including Washington's National Zoological Park, is expected to end in two to three weeks with 20 to 35 indictments, according to sources close to the case. The two-year investigation, which has ranged around the world, including Australia, Thailand, Ceylon, Singapore, France and Switzerland, is now before a federal grand jury in Philadelphia.... One

U.S. government source involved in the prosecution called it "the most important wildlife case ever."

The government indicted Molt an incredible six different times, meaning he had to face six different criminal judges, in six different cases. Half a dozen of his American accomplices were indicted, along with his alleged partners in Singapore, Kenya, France, and Switzerland. Among the latter was Jonathan Leakey, son of famed archaeologists Louis and Mary Leakey, older brother of Kenya's antipoaching warrior Richard, and owner of an East African reptile and amphibian export company called Jonathan Leakey Limited.

To thwart investigators, one of Molt's team killed dozens of illegal reptiles and buried the evidence in the New Jersey Pine Barrens. Agent O'Kane dug that evidence up and placed it in jars of formaldehyde. The case was horrible, but it was also stepping on some toes. It wasn't long before expenses, time, and political pressure from exposing the National Zoo combined in a way that threatened the investigators' careers. They were told to stop.

Lead investigator Joe O'Kane was an Irishman, raised in Philadelphia's Kensington section, the area famous for its second-story thieves, where growing up it wasn't unusual to get a knock on your door and open it to find a large boy saying, "Your little brother said you could beat me up." It was through those moments and dozens of similar battles that bigger kids in O'Kane's neighborhood learned that Joe O'Kane liked to fight. O'Kane understood his bosses' frustration. *Who could like reptiles?* O'Kane didn't like reptiles. *But if you could make a case for something so low,* he decided, *then everything else would benefit.* Harvard-educated prosecutor Tom Mellon took a more intellectual approach to the Molt case: they were dealing with a concept, not a Philadelphia reptile smuggler. Wildlife was disappearing forever because no one would push old law to stop new threats. When O'Kane's superior in Washington, D.C., still did not grasp Mellon's point, the lawyer explained his position more plainly: "Your laws aren't worth the fucking paper they're written on," he said. Mellon would no more back down from the Molt fight than would O'Kane.

It was the 1970s, the decade of environmental activism. The CITES treaty was brand-new. The Endangered Species Act had hardly been tested. No one had wielded the Lacey Act the way Mellon thought it could be used. Molt's prosecution was to be a showstopper.

Molt showed up for the first trial wearing one black sock and one gray one. He held his hand up and swore to tell the truth, then forgot to put his hand down until the judge reminded him. He did everything he could think of to convey his innocence, and after court adjourned each day, he went home, opened his mail, and took in more smuggled reptiles.

He devastated the prosecution. Through his lawyers, Molt attacked the government on the grounds of unconstitutionality, tardiness, illegal search, and a host of other objections. He embarrassed prosecutors with testimony stating that the secretary of the interior, Cecil Andrus, dined regularly at Dominique's, a trendy French Washington, D.C., restaurant famous for serving exotic wildlife, including, according to *Time* magazine, Pennsylvania's endangered timber rattlesnake. Most damaging of all, Judge J. William Ditter Jr. agreed with Molt that the search of his filing cabinet, done without a search warrant, had violated Molt's constitutional rights. All the letters, invoices, and recorded phone conversations the agents had seized were thrown out.

Molt beat the government back and even made new law when Judge Herbert A. Fogel interpreted the Lacey Act more narrowly than it ever had been before. Fogel's decision was upheld on appeal. As a result, Hank Molt weakened the Lacey Act, the government's most important legal weapon for combating wildlife smuggling.

What may have helped Molt most was a decision by Tom Mellon's boss, U.S. Attorney David W. Marston, not to prosecute America's zoos. The burden of proof was too high, he told reporters. To be successful, prosecutors would have had to prove that the zoo curators knew they were violating both the Lacey Act *and* foreign law when buying reptiles from Molt. It was impossible to show criminal intent given the circumstances, and the zoos might have genuinely been ignorant of Molt's methods.

The entire zoo world got a pass, and so when it came time to sentence Molt on the charges he had not beaten, the judge commented on the imbalance in his courtroom and gave Molt a light sentence: three months in federal prison. Historically, it was still a significant prison term. The year Molt was indicted there were 584 convictions for similar wildlife crimes, resulting in a total of ten days of prison time. The average defendant in a wildlife case paid fifty bucks and went home.

Molt's story triggered an international sensation. Newspapers around the world covered it. *National Geographic* called Molt's case "the most celebrated wildlife case so far." The *Atlantic* later cited Molt's case as the one that gave the government "the first clear idea of the complexity and sweep of illegal wildlife activity." Because of Molt, a firestorm over wildlife crime erupted within the federal government, beginning with the president.

On August 2, 1979, President Jimmy Carter announced that a "massive" illegal trade in wildlife had been uncovered. In response, he directed the Justice Department to establish a new wildlife section staffed with lawyers "who will be trained to be wildlife law enforcement specialists." He also directed the Departments of Agriculture, Commerce, the Interior, the Treasury, and Justice to investigate illegal wildlife trade aggressively and to prosecute violators as white-collar criminals. The man behind the Carter directive was Assistant Attorney General James W. Moorman, who believed that when a disaster came along you had to take advantage of it. The recent Love Canal catastrophe in New York had galvanized the country to the dangers of hazardous waste, and had enabled the administration to push through new protections at the EPA. Moorman considered the Molt case "the Love Canal of wildlife crimes." He used Molt as a poster child for why the Justice Department needed a new centralized unit to advise federal prosecutors around the country on how to attack wildlife criminals.

To set up the new wildlife section, Moorman tapped Kenneth Berlin, a thirty-two-year-old corporate lawyer from New York who had attended the very first CITES meeting, had been active in fisheries law, and was a serious bird-watcher. Berlin set up the Justice Department's new Wildlife and Marine Resources Section and took on responsibility for the interagency wildlife enforcement program also called for by the president. The need to get agencies talking to one another was glaring. For example, when the Department of Agriculture seized smuggled birds, it ground them up to prevent the spread of deadly Newcastle disease, destroying evidence needed by U.S. Fish and Wildlife investigators and by federal prosecutors. Customs agents generally enjoyed wildlife cases, but many at the U.S. Fish and Wildlife Service seemed hesitant to take on responsibility for policing imported wildlife, especially since the maximum criminal penalty for smuggling was only a misdemeanor. *Why break your neck over a misdemeanor?*

Berlin had two goals for the future: to convince the heads of U.S. Fish and Wildlife, U.S. Customs, and other agencies to take wildlife-smuggling cases seriously, and to do the same with federal judges.

In the coming years, the wildlife section Moorman and Berlin launched would become a hands-on brain trust both for strategizing and for prosecuting complex wildlife cases. Thirteen years later it would be a model for prosecutor Chris McAliley's vision for Miami, and not long after that it would play a role in Mike Van Nostrand's life.

Molt's impact on Washington did not end with the White House. In 1981, Congress amended the Lacey Act, lowering the burden of proof cited by Philadelphia's chief federal prosecutor as having been too high to allow pursuit of America's zoo curators. In its report accompanying the newly amended law, the U.S. Senate named Molt as the reason for its amendment extending the Lacey Act's reach when it came to smugglers violating foreign laws (effectively reversing Judge Fogel's decision). Perhaps most reflective of all regarding the government's opinion of Hank Molt, Congress increased the Lacey Act's criminal penalty from a misdemeanor to a felony.

For AUSA Mellon, Molt's case would nag as an unsatisfying moment in an illustrious career. Like Chris McAliley, he endured ribbing for taking on reptiles; one judge called the idea "egregious." Unaware of the revolution in wildlife prosecutions his effort initiated, Mellon would move on to become chief of the office's criminal division, and later to private practice. Likewise, in 1976, freshly returned from their global investigation, Agent O'Kane grew a beard, declaring, "I'm not going to shave until we win the case." He wears a beard to this day.

Molt served his time at Allenwood federal prison. Using the pay phone, he continued to smuggle reptiles while incarcerated. His only mistake, he believed, was that he'd unlocked his filing cabinet and let customs agents see his paperwork. If he could have that day back, he knew exactly what he would say to Agent O'Kane. Sitting recently in a bar in Charlotte, North Carolina, recounting a life as an "international criminal, a rogue, and a pirate," Molt shared the response he would give today: "I'd say, 'Your mother's a fucking whore, get your scummy moth-erfucking ass out of my fucking shop. Get the fuck out of here right now! I'll call the fucking cops—or fucking take me down!'"

He believes the best thing that ever happened to him was his trial and the resulting publicity. When he got out of prison he was contacted by a man in Ohio who had read about him in a recent *National Geographic* piece entitled "Wild Cargo: The Business of Smuggling Animals," the article featuring Mr. Dang and his albino Burmese python. Edmund F. Celebucki did not know a lot about reptiles or smuggling, he told Molt, but he'd like to learn. "You're on," Molt said, and the two began one of Molt's best smuggling runs ever.

Molt and Celebucki would smuggle together, open a sex club together, and bring in Australian species never before seen in the United States. Three U.S. zoos would win prestigious Edward H. Bean Awards for breeding rare python species reportedly imported by Molt. The founder stock of seventeen other reptile species would likewise come from him. Molt would continue to make a living as a smuggler and a dealer in venomous snakes, but the zoo market Molt had once known was gone. Stung by their association, many curators treated him as a pariah.

Molt had ruled the 1970s as a reptile smuggler. He did a bit of time, fought the law, and established a new principle for a top-level international reptile smuggler: *Never quit.* He had opened and closed the era of the zoo collector. "You're only as good as the snakes in your cage" he believed. There was a time when he had the snakes. Then there was a time when Tom Crutchfield had the snakes. The next era would go to the smuggler who could bring in rarities the way Molt could, find breedable animals the way Crutchfield had, and do it all on the sort of scale Ray Van Nostrand had established.

Out of the same gun, as Molt liked to put it, came a second bullet. That bullet had a son. Wildlife prosecutors in Miami and in Washington, D.C., would soon have a chance to test themselves against Mike Van Nostrand. And so would Agent Bepler. In fact, Van Nostrand was getting ready for them.

Jungle Cartel

Patrick O'Brien was struggling, looking for any business he could get, when Mike Van Nostrand's truck pulled up outside his law office for the first time. O'Brien had gone nights to the University of Miami School of Law, graduating cum laude when he was forty-eight years old. Now he was fifty-one, with a master's degree in criminal justice, an undergraduate degree in physics, and a plaque somewhere to remind him that he had already retired once. He wasn't ready to do it again. The Miami branch of the law firm Greenberg, Traurig had hired him as "of counsel." It sounded good, but in reality "of counsel" was legalese for purgatory. It was a title law firms gave to aging partners they wanted to put out to pasture, or retired senators they hoped would make some rain; it was a position they gave nonlawyer engineers to help the firm's patent and trademark practice, or senior associates they could not bring themselves to fire. Being of counsel was very much like being held back again in school: you looked a lot older than the kids around you, you understood a lot more than they did, but everyone in the building knew you lacked something important needed to make it to the next grade. In O'Brien's case, that something was a proven record of landing clients who paid.

O'Brien had just finished twenty-six years as a special agent with the U.S. Customs Service, including a stint as special agent in charge for South Florida and the Caribbean. His expertise was money laundering and drug smuggling. Greenberg, Traurig had recruited him to build them a customs practice. Customs law is a very lucrative field if you work in Washington, D.C., where someone might pay you to convince the Court of International Trade that a Rollerblade is a shoe and not a skate, but down in Miami with the go-fast boats and the automatic weapons, customs law was a walk-in business worth about five grand per. To make it at a firm like Greenberg, Traurig, that meant O'Brien had to bring in three new clients a week, every week, starting a number of weeks ago.

Van Nostrand took a chair. O'Brien listened as Mike described the reptile wholesale business, his history with the U.S. Fish and Wildlife Service, and his situation with an agent named Bepler. The government had just filed a fifty-seven-count civil penalty action against Mike for $613,000.

The suit did not mention any names, but it was obvious, Van Nostrand said, who the government's source was. It had been a year since Medina's arrest. All fifty-seven counts related to reptiles from Argentina allegedly smuggled between May 1, 1991, and the exact date of

Medina's arrest, March 25, 1992. The suit was broken down by species and by trip, five trips in 1992 alone, almost as if Medina had kept a diary every time he'd traveled.

O'Brien tried to focus on the law, but the agent inside him was astounded at Bepler's handling of Medina. He *arrested* the guy *at the airport*? A controlled delivery was standard operating procedure anytime you caught a mule in transit. You rolled him and thirty minutes later he was back on his way to land you the real fish. Bepler's mistake was absolutely inexcusable, and one he would have crucified an agent for under his command. *Fish and Wildlife!*

The filing of a civil penalty action meant the government probably lacked enough evidence for a criminal case. That was good. Given the reputation of U.S. Fish and Wildlife, it was possible they had already given up on the criminal front altogether. Still, they could pursue both avenues at the same time, a little like the way the U.S. attorney for Brooklyn had just announced he was proceeding with John Gotti.

Van Nostrand's troubles with U.S. Fish and Wildlife included more recent problems, too. Agent Bepler had just seized an African lizard shipment. Mike seemed to think Bepler had it in for him because of how big and successful he was.

O'Brien looked the twenty-seven-year-old reptile dealer over. Even negotiating it down, half a million dollars in civil penalties was a hell of a lot of green iguanas. Who knew whether Strictly Reptiles could sustain a hit like that. O'Brien agreed to take on the African lizard case. He set his fee at $5,000 and asked for half of his money up front. He wasn't sure if a kid in the reptile business would be worth it over the long haul to Greenberg, Traurig, but at least Strictly Reptiles would mean one less customs case he had to find that week.

After their meeting, O'Brien completed the firm's client-intake forms. One was a conflict-of-interest form, and another was for the firm's marketing people. O'Brien had the tight smile of an ex-cop. In the line on the form that asked for a new client's "Interesting Aspects," he scribbled: "We are helping this creep who imports lizards captured in a small valley in Tanzania so he can sell them to kids who put them in cages."

Only later would he come to understand the size of the reptile industry and the diversity and magnitude of Strictly Reptiles' illegal activity. Soon the fledgling lawyer would be getting work from New York, Chicago, and Los Angeles, as well as from other wildlife companies in Florida—all with ties to Strictly Reptiles. O'Brien had just signed up his biggest client for several years to come. His financial troubles were over for good.

Van Nostrand was pleased to have a lawyer on his side. He did not need O'Brien because he was confused about the law; he knew the law. Really, wildlife law was not difficult to grasp. It all came down to one sentence: *The less you know, the better you are.* The only law with any real jail time behind it was the Lacey Act, and the Lacey Act required proof that a buyer knew that animals he'd purchased were illegal. So Mike had a golden rule: Ask no questions. If he asked no questions, his smugglers could tell him all the lies they wanted. Lies were just fine with him.

If a guy walked in with a suitcase full of tortoises,

set them on the floor, and said he wanted fifty bucks apiece for them, that's what he got. But if that same guy said anything else, if he said the tortoises lacked papers or he wished he could breed them, if he mentioned what the temperature was in Buenos Aires, then that tortoise seller went out the door, often with a stream of profanity in his wake. Because even if the guy wasn't a setup when he came in the door, if he got popped down the road you could be sure he was going to rat out Strictly Reptiles—as Medina had.

Van Nostrand wanted a good lawyer for two reasons. First, to handle the civil action against him, and second, to get a fight started. Bepler and the rest of Fish and Wildlife needed to know they could not just walk into his shop and take his stuff. He intended to fight Bepler and anybody else who challenged him, no matter what.

Hiring O'Brien took some pressure off Mike, and he thought maybe it would even get his nosebleeds to stop. It was definitely going to make his trip to Southeast Asia easier. He had never been there before, but now he had a chance to earn some real money. Bepler would croak if he knew who Mike planned to see. In a way, knowing Bepler was after him made the trip that much more special.

One year after Medina's arrest and just days after being informed of a $613,000 lawsuit, Van Nostrand was in the air. He hated to fly. Even in business class he was too big for the seats and, more to the point, he was just not an "international" guy. When he was first starting out he had traveled to Africa to see his supplier there. "Black is black," the man had said to him. You did not change what you could not change. Mike did not want to change at all. He liked watching baseball, spending time at home with Michelle. They were talking about starting a family. It would be great, some boys to play catch with. Michelle loved all living things—birds, cats, turtles, dogs. To him, pets were money. Worse, pets were money that died. He was what the bunny huggers said he was: he was a flesh peddler.

Two men controlled the live reptile trade out of Southeast Asia. Keng Liang "Anson" Wong lived in Malaysia, and Mohamad Hardi lived in Indonesia. Mike intended to see them both. He brought his employee Dale Marantz with him. He had to bring somebody, and Marantz was already up to his knees in Medina. Marantz was one of his father's so-called "friends," a drug dealer as well as a reptile person, the kind of man who would show up at the side door to the garage back when Mike was a boy. He hated how men like Dale always seemed to find his father and get him into trouble. Guys like Dale didn't have to actually do anything—just being around and willing was enough to raise Van Nostrand's blood pressure.

Marantz was worried. The government had sued him, too, for his role as the link between Van Nostrand and Medina. The penalty against Marantz was only $35,000. Negotiated down, it was going to be pennies, probably less than Van Nostrand had at home in his sock drawer. But just because they shared a common problem didn't mean Mike wanted to listen to Marantz complain all the way to Malaysia, and he let Marantz know it.

People said Mike was rude, that he screamed a lot, and he did. But if he didn't yell and push people back, who would do it? *His father?* Everybody loved "Big Ray."

"Pops" they called his father, too. Anytime somebody asked for "Big Ray" Mike knew he was about to lose money. Guys drove by staring at the cars in the parking lot trying to see if Ray was in before taking a chance at stopping by. Complete strangers walked in asking, "Is Ray here?"

Mike would offer a guy a godfather deal on a $3,500 Aldabra tortoise, knock it down to $2,700, say, and the first thing the guy would ask was does he get his 10 percent "friend of Ray" cut, too? People believed Ray was the company's soft spot. They were right, too. Mike was rude to people because somebody had to set limits and it wasn't going to be "Pops."

After a grueling flight they landed on Malaysia's turtle-shaped island of Penang, home to Anson Wong. If Van Nostrand had to pick only one, the most important person in the international reptile business would have to be Anson. He controlled the live reptile trade out of Malaysia and, with the exception of Indonesia, out of most of Southeast Asia, too. And that was not all.

Wildlife dealers, zoos, and museums all over the world knew that if they could pay for it, Anson could probably get it for them. Africa, South America—it didn't matter. Wong could get anything: snow leopard pelts, panda skins, rhino horns. He had operations in Vietnam. He raised tigers to be stuffed and sold as trophy mounts. On one occasion he'd offered Mike a Spix's macaw. The Spix's macaw was the *Mona Lisa* of the illegal bird world, the rarest bird on the planet. According to some studies, the Spix's macaw did not exist. It was extinct. Anson was asking $100,000 for his. He had three of them.

Wong's true specialty was endangered and seldom-imported CITES Appendix I and II reptiles. He supplied Mike—as he had supplied Ray—with reptiles from the Fiji Islands, Indonesia, Australia, Madagascar, the Seychelles, India, Sri Lanka, South Africa, Pakistan, China, Vietnam, the Philippines, and Thailand. When Vietnam was shut down to trade, Anson had been *the* source for two of the most popular pets in the reptile business: Burmese pythons and Chinese water dragons. He got them out of Vietnam and laundered tens of thousands of them through Thailand and Malaysia. Without Anson's work over the past decade, there would have been no Strictly Reptiles.

Wong's driver met Van Nostrand and Marantz at the Penang airport and drove them to one of the luxury tourist hotels overlooking the Strait of Malacca. Van Nostrand did not intend to stay in Asia long. He and Wong had a smuggling project going that Van Nostrand wanted to expand; after that he had some special animals he wanted to get from Indonesia before heading home. Like his father, Mike had no real interest in "exotic" travel. His interest was money, and he planned to make a lot of it based on this trip.

Before bed, Mike shared a rare drink at the bar with Marantz. He did not do drugs, even marijuana. Drugs had taken his father away, almost forever, and he treated them accordingly. He had nothing against alcohol; he just didn't drink it anymore. He didn't have time.

The next morning Wong's driver picked them up and

took them to see Wong. Anson was a slight, baby-faced man who wore large eyeglasses and spoke with a British accent—from studying in England, Van Nostrand had heard. He was only thirty-five, eight years older than Mike. Wong had the relaxed air of an intellectual, of an artist maybe, but with a focus of something else.

While Van Nostrand was a tactician, Wong was a grand strategist. He sold an animal, its capture, the mode of delivery, and the financing, much as one might sell a movie project or a skyscraper. And, he boasted, when he did not get paid he had contacts who were familiar with debt collection. What Mike liked most about Anson was his ego. Wong believed there was nobody in the world as big as he was, and he was probably right.

Like Van Nostrand, Wong had a father in the reptile business. The elder Wong had raised alligators for skins. Anson was the first of two sons, a fourth-generation Chinese in Malaysia. After high school Anson had left Penang for mainland Malaysia, were he'd tried his hand as a dolphin trainer at Johor Safari Park. He'd soon transferred to parrots because the dolphins kept splashing water on his eyeglasses.

Through trips to the wet market to buy food for the safari park's animals, Wong met wildlife collectors and foreign zoo people. He discovered there was money to be made exporting wildlife, and soon he opened his own company, Exotic Skins and Alives.

Now Wong owned a well-regarded zoo on Penang, as well as an animal-export company called Sungai Rusa Wildlife.

Van Nostrand was surprised at Wong's headquarters. It was small. From the outside it could have been a hair salon;

the inside was nothing more than a desk in a little room at the back of a small building, cluttered with shipping boxes and a few cheap desks. There were invoices everywhere, and some maps on the walls. His wife helped run an interior design company, which specialized in modernist corporate and residential interiors. Mies van der Rohe Pavilion chairs, antelope-legged Le Corbusier–type end tables—Bauhaus school designs were an odd product to sell on an island known for its spices and tropical beaches, but Penang's economy had always been bipolar.

According to legend, after purchasing Penang on behalf of the British East India Company, the only way Captain Francis Light could get natives to clear the island to build a fort was to load his ship's cannons with silver dollars and fire them into the jungle. Thus did commercial ingenuity level the island's jungles well enough to establish Penang's first settlement, followed two centuries later by Dell, Intel, and a host of international companies in pursuit of money on an island cleared of its regulatory underbrush.

A pilgrimage to see Wong was a rite of passage for America's top reptile smugglers. Five years earlier, Tom Crutchfield had made the trip. Things had not turned out so well for Crutchfield, however. He was arrested for smuggling Fiji banded iguanas from Wong shortly after he returned home. The case was still going on, but already it was looking to be a greater mockery of the American judicial system than Hank Molt's had been a decade and a half earlier. The Tampa-based prosecutor was an amateur herpetologist, and you could not be a serious herpetologist in Florida, amateur or not, without being a customer of Crutchfield's. The prosecutor was personally involved in the case and, eventually, would go so far overboard with irrelevant allegations that before it was over, the Eleventh Circuit Court of Appeals would find him "guilty of multiple and continuing instances of intentional misconduct," reverse Crutchfield's conviction, and order a new trial. Only then would Crutchfield plead guilty.

Wong had been indicted in the Crutchfield case, too, and believed he would be arrested if he entered the United States. He didn't seem worried, though. When he wanted to visit the country, he flew to Canada and drove across the border. Malaysia had no extradition treaty with the United States—not that it would have mattered, anyway. He had friends in the Malaysian government. There was no way he could operate as he did without them. He was invincible, and he loved it.

"There's the right way and the Wong way," he liked to say, along with a line Van Nostrand loved to use himself: "Laws are made to be broken."

His smuggling methods were as diverse as the species he sold. Wong did the usual, of course. He stuffed rare Madagascan tortoises into black socks and hid them in the dark bottoms of shipping crates. He used what he called "cover animals," large wild-caught monitor lizards, or biting Tokay geckos, or rear-fanged mangrove snakes; he placed them on top of illegal animals, ready to spring. He built crates with hidden compartments. He labeled endangered but harmless animals "venomous," and called protected snakes "tree vipers." Malaysia shares borders with Indonesia, Singapore, and Thailand, and he exported animals smuggled from those countries, saying they were caught domestically. He employed more advanced methods, too; these he sold as "projects."

Wong had a scheme for laundering Indian star tortoises through the United Arab Emirates and Malaysia to the United States. Indian star tortoises are beautiful little dark brown batting helmets painted in a kaleidoscope of bamboo yellow shapes that really do resemble stars. They were illegal to export from their range states—India, Pakistan, and Sri Lanka—and they were also protected by CITES. Without an Appendix II export permit, the United States would not let them into the country.

Wong's plan exploited a major exception in the CITES treaty for captive-bred wildlife. CITES allowed trade in captive-bred animals, in some cases, even rare species. The important point for Wong and Van Nostrand was that you could "captive-breed" an animal almost anywhere in the world, which meant you were not beholden to India, Pakistan, or Sri Lanka to explain where you got your Indian star tortoises. All you needed to turn an illegally poached Indian star tortoise into a "legal" one was a government official somewhere in the world to say your animal had been captive-born in their country, and stamp your paperwork.

Which was where the UAE government came in.

Wong and Van Nostrand had tried their plan a few times, and it worked well enough that Van Nostrand wanted to increase the operation. Van Nostrand did not know where Wong was poaching the star tortoises from, and he did not want to know. The less he knew, the better. According to their paperwork, the tortoises were captive-bred at a farm in Dubai, shipped to Wong, and then reexported to Strictly Reptiles. It was expensive routing poached tortoises through the UAE and Malaysia, and it took an extra CITES stamp, but Mike figured Wong probably did it to control the operation. In any case, it was worth it. Wong had the same UAE laundering scheme going with customers in France and Japan.

Malaysian law gave Wong an extraordinary advantage. Malaysia did not protect turtle species inside its borders. Under a twist in the law, if you could get star tortoises into Malaysia, you could sell them at will. It was, Wong said, because the royal families collected turtle eggs "for their aphrodisiac" and so could not prohibit the rest of the people from indulging. In any case, the notably strong laws that led to high prices for species smuggled out of nearby countries like Australia, New Zealand, and the Philippines made Penang the best turtle-laundering point in the world.

The most memorable part of Van Nostrand's short visit to Penang was the drive to Wong's mountaintop home. Mike gawked at the drop off some of the turns. "You got to be crazy!" he shouted. The road to Wong's house was so steep and so narrow that once you started up the mountain you had to go all the way to the top. You couldn't turn around, no matter how much you wanted to.

They ironed out their plans to step up their Indian star tortoise project. With Crutchfield in trouble, Van Nostrand expected his business with Anson to increase. After a lunch of shark's-fin soup and a visit to the Penang Butterfly Farm, Van Nostrand and Marantz got back on an airplane and headed for Jakarta, and the main purpose of their trip.

With more than thirteen thousand islands, each home to its own variety of species, Indonesia is the jewelry store of the reptile world. It has borders with Papua New Guinea and is a stone's throw from Australia—both home to rare and protected species. Considering the region as a whole, Indonesia is not just a jewelry store, it is the anchor unit in the world's most exclusive shopping mall. The main reptile-exporting company in Indonesia was Firma Hasco, owned by Mohamad Hardi. A small man with a ferocious laugh, Hardi had followed his father into the bird business, expanding over the years into reptiles.

Van Nostrand had traveled halfway around the world to see Hardi and to bring home two python species, either of which would fund his trip many times over. He intended to smuggle both species home, in two very different ways.

In contrast to the personal attention Wong had given them, Van Nostrand and Marantz spent most of their time in Jakarta with Firma Hasco's manager, Andre Van Meer, a Dutch reptile expert who had moved to Indonesia to work for Hardi. Each morning, Van Meer would pick up Van Nostrand and Marantz at their hotel and take them to Firma Hasco's holding farm to pick out reptiles.

In the reptile world, there is green and then there is green. Green tree pythons are beautiful enough that from time to time when a corporation wants to add an exotic touch to an advertising campaign, the species its executives choose is often the green tree python. They are also common in zoo collections and are almost always seen the way they spend their daytime existence: wrapped in a coil the size of a dinner plate with their heads dead center, looped over a tree branch, like a braided emerald rug on a clothesline. At night they rely on heat-sensitive labial pits to find prey in the dark.

To high-end collectors not all green tree pythons

are alike. Locked onto islands, green tree pythons have evolved distinctive patterns and coloring according to their locality. Much as a coin collector might assemble a "set" of different years of the same coin design, collectors of green tree pythons often assemble a variety of "locality type" animals within a single species. The most valuable green tree pythons of the moment were found on the Indonesian island of Aru. "Arus" were characterized by a broken series of white dots along the spine, with licks of sky blue at the edges of the spots and along the lips. In the best specimens, the underbelly was also sky blue. Housed in an acrylic display box (much as a large porcelain doll might be) with a pair of branches to hang on, even a single animal was a showpiece. Collectors paid a great deal for Arus. A shipment of fifty nice adults was worth $75,000.

Firma Hasco supplied Van Nostrand with a CITES permit to export fifty captive-bred green tree pythons. Van Nostrand spent each day picking through the wild-caught pythons hunters and middlemen brought to the farm. If he was going to charge top dollar, he wanted top-quality specimens. The permit itself was illegal, of course. In 1993, nobody in Indonesia was *breeding* green tree pythons. Even if they were, his were straight out of the hunters' bags. Hasco was not breeding green tree pythons, but that was a matter of perspective. It was not reptiles Van Nostrand was buying anymore; it was paperwork.

Van Nostrand found the snakes he was looking for. To him, buying under a false permit was not a crime. There was no such thing as a false permit. If the government gave you a permit it was like your schoolteacher giving you a hall pass. The permit meant it was okay. That you paid the government official for his or her signature was no different from paying a maître d' for seating you without a dinner reservation.

As long as he had CITES paperwork—forged paperwork, fraudulent paperwork, but paperwork—Van Nostrand knew Bepler could not touch him. It was ironic: the system CITES had created to protect animals also protected him.

That was something Bepler ought to have thought about. CITES, the Endangered Species Act, the Lacey Act—the more laws they put on the books, the more rare an animal became in the marketplace. The number of people willing to break laws to collect animals was small, giving a monopoly to those willing to take the risk. In the animal business *rare* and *protected* amounted to the same thing; one designation was biological, the other regulatory, but both pointed to a scarcity—which meant supply was limited. It did not take a degree from Broward Community College to figure out the result: protecting an animal elevated its market price, sometimes through the roof.

The boy who'd wanted to be an accountant was finally out of the reptile business. It might not be balance sheets and income statements he was working with, but CITES documents were still very much financial documents. He was growing to hate Bepler, but he did owe him a thank-you. Bepler and his laws were the reason he was going to make so much money on this trip. All he needed was the paperwork.

And air-conditioning. The accommodations in Jakarta were not as comfortable as the hotel in Penang. Van Nostrand spent his days in the hot sun, working through animals. He picked out crocodile monitors—the world's longest lizards, capable of slicing open a man's arm with their claws—and he selected fat, ground-dwelling blood pythons and reticulated pythons, the world's longest snake. It wasn't true that he "didn't like" reptiles; he just felt no remorse bagging them up for sale. If he didn't sell them, some skin trader would turn them into a handbag, so even if he didn't love reptiles the way some PETA advocate said he should, he was pretty sure reptiles liked him a little better than his alternative. Van Nostrand had dinner with Hardi during the trip, but he preferred the company of Andre Van Meer. He and Van Meer were close to the same age. They worked together throughout the week.

Van Meer, whose friends called him "Dre," had grown up in Breda, Holland. He started raising crickets and mealworms to sell as reptile food, and before he knew it, his hobby turned into a full-time business. During a trip to Indonesia to meet some of the world's biggest reptile suppliers in person, he'd been offered a couple of opportunities to work for reptile exporters. He chose Hardi because of his connections in government.

The most valuable species Van Nostrand acquired from his host was the Timor python. Endemic to Indonesia, the mustard-and-brown python was a very rare snake in the pet trade and worth about $2,000 apiece. Van Nostrand purchased nine baby Timor pythons. They came without paperwork, so as he and Marantz prepared to leave they had to decide how to get them by U.S. Customs.

Van Nostrand wanted to carry the Timor pythons back in his carry-on bag, simple and clean, but Marantz insisted on putting the snakes in socks and strapping them to his legs with Ace bandages. During their layover at Singapore's Changi Airport, he and Marantz went into a bathroom to check on the snakes and discovered that two were dead, suffocated under the bandages. That was $4,000 out the window.

They boarded their connecting flight, and out over the Pacific Ocean Marantz began to worry. Because of Medina, their names might be in the Customs Service's database. "What if we're red-flagged?" he asked Van Nostrand.

The closer they got to the United States, the more worried Marantz became. "They're going to stop us," he said.

Van Nostrand turned to him. Marantz was sweating. His face was red. *"Man,"* Van Nostrand hissed at him, "we're gonna go to jail! Look at you. You are *not* good. Gimme them snakes!"

Marantz had transferred the snakes to his carry-on bag. Van Nostrand grabbed the bag and a sweat sock and took them into the airplane toilet. He put the baby pythons in the sock, and he put the sock in his pants. People think too much, he said to himself.

He walked through U.S. Customs with the pythons in his shorts.

Two weeks after his return, with Bepler's lawsuit hardly a month old, Van Nostrand decided to move his company. He bought an enormous warehouse from the Frito-Lay company. It came with two loading bays, no windows, and two ironies. First, it was one lot over from the dinky little Joy gas station storefront he and his mother had first moved to several years ago. Second, it was virtually straight down the street from Chip Bepler's house. Anytime Chip, as Van Nostrand now knew him, wanted to take his wife to Hollywood Beach, he would have to drive right by Strictly Reptiles. Bepler wanted to sue him? Van Nostrand took almost all the money Bepler wanted in his $613,000 lawsuit and sank it into his new facility.

If Mike thought things could not go any better, he was wrong. The movie *Jurassic Park* came out. Reptiles on a scale nobody had ever seen before, busting out of one enclosure after another, all in the name of profit—it was art imitating life all over again. A reporter from the *Miami Herald* came to interview Strictly Reptiles, self-described as the world's largest wholesaler of green iguanas, about "the iguana craze" the movie had spawned. Ray's girlfriend chalked the boom up to people in apartments not being allowed to keep dogs. Others were not so pleased with the film's impact. "That stupid movie that made everybody crazy about reptiles" was what the head of Costa Rica's Green Iguana Foundation called it.

Just as *Jurassic Park* hit theaters, a wooden crate arrived at Miami International Airport. It contained half a dozen strange lizards, listed on the import declaration as *Chlamydosaurus kingii*.

Wildlife inspectors at Miami International looked up the species name and saw that the lizards were native to New Guinea and Australia, but not to Malaysia, which is where the paperwork indicated they came from. "Frilled dragons don't come from Malaysia," the inspector told Van Nostrand.

"Well, brown basilisks don't occur in Florida," he shot back, "but they're all over the place. It's an introduced species!"

The lizard was said to be the model for *Jurassic Park*'s dilophosaurus, a dinosaur that did actually exist but did not (so far as is known) spit venom, and also did not explode a terrifying umbrella from its neck the way the lizard Anson Wong sent did. Miami cleared the lizards. It was Van Nostrand's first time dealing in frilled dragons, the reptile emblem of Australia and a species protected throughout its range

Van Nostrand priced his first group at $1,500 apiece. He sold them all. He needed more.

For his second trip to Indonesia that year he took his wife, Michelle, along. It was just before Christmas, and the trip would be part work, and part pleasure. He wanted to pick out another shipment, and there were other things he wanted to say to Andre Van Meer that he did not want to discuss over the telephone. It was not that he was afraid of Bepler—it was next to impossible to get wiretap authority for a wildlife crime—but there was no sense in being stupid.

He had control and he wanted to keep it. In fact, that is what he spoke to Dre about: control. There was a way to structure sale of this new lizard using Indonesia, Malaysia, and Europe that could make all of them a great deal of money. "Here is the law," he told Van Meer, laying his hand on a table like a knife, "and"—moving his hand a few inches—"here is me." It took knowing the law on three continents and in half a dozen countries for the operation to work. They agreed to do it.

Next, Van Nostrand picked out legal animals from Firma Hasco's collection. He wanted a really big water monitor. Water monitors are slightly smaller versions of their relative the Komodo dragon. Hasco's were housed in outdoor walk-in pens. At five-eleven and over 320 pounds, Van Nostrand was too big to fit through the door of the pen to pick the lizard he wanted. A young Indonesian man went in, and Van Nostrand directed him. The Indonesian made eye contact with one of the giant lizards, which thrashed its tail. Instantly the whole pen was alive with swatting tails and snapping jaws. The Indonesian jumped onto a tree branch. Eventually the animals calmed down enough so that the young man could try to corral the lizard Van Nostrand wanted. By this time, Dre had heard the racket.

"I'll get it," Dre said, and reached down just as the monitor's head appeared in the doorway. Instead of grabbing the monitor's neck, Dre thrust his fingers into the lizard's mouth. The monitor headed out of the cage, dragging Dre around by his fingers. Men had to use a two-by-four to pry the lizard's mouth open.

Before the Van Nostrands left, Dre took them to the Jakarta zoo. The reptile collection was abysmal, probably not worth more than five grand for the whole row, but the orangutans were fascinating. There was just something about the way they moved, giant red men flying through trees. As Van Nostrand stood and watched them, a crowd of Indonesians gathered nearby. They were gesturing and taking photographs, but not of the orangutans. "What are they pointing at?" he asked. Van Meer laughed. "They have never seen a human being as big as you," he said. Some got their pictures taken next to him.

Van Nostrand had left his father in charge of the business while he was in Asia. Ray worried about his son.

Mike took everything much too seriously. It was a game, he'd told him more than once; he had to see it as a game. When a customer makes you an offer, you make a counter-offer. But that's not how Mike was. If a guy made him an offer he didn't like, he refused to speak to him.

What happened? his father might ask.

He offered me forty-five bucks for the baby blood python. I told him to get the fuck out.

What are you asking on them?

Sixty-five.

Would you take fifty?

Yeah, Mike would say. Fifty's all right. Ray would have to go find the guy and sell him the snake. Maybe for forty-eight, because of the trouble...

Mike had started gaining weight after Ray went to prison. By the time Ray got out, his son was much bigger. He was biting his fingernails a lot. And he was getting these nosebleeds. The kid had never done a drug in his life and he was getting nosebleeds. It wasn't natural.

Negotiating over animals was not the only way Ray and Mike differed. Covering yourself with paperwork was not Ray's style, either. When he saw something he liked, he went after it. That's what it was all about. Besides, they were making so much money, why not have some fun?

Like the rock iguanas. "That's very pretty," Ray said one day, pointing to a photograph of a rare Bahamian iguana, the Sandy Cay rock iguana, *Cyclura rileyi cristata*.

Dwayne Cunningham nodded. He was a reptile lover and a professional comedian who worked cruise lines in the Caribbean. "You like that one, Ray?" he asked.

"Beautiful," Ray said, his eyes sparkling the same pale

blue that flecked the lizard's body. He had never seen the lizard before. Almost nobody had.

On the basis of little more than a nod from Ray, Cunningham and a snorkeling instructor for Norwegian Cruise Lines flew to the Bahamas, rented a Zodiac, camped out for two nights, caught sixteen extremely rare iguanas using nooses tied to fishing poles, stuffed the lizards into their dive bags, and deadheaded back to Miami on the cruise ship the *Norway*.

Cunningham waited for a Saturday, when Mike was least likely to be in the shop, before bringing some of the iguanas to Ray.

When Mike found out, he had a fit. This was not the tree-climbing, pet-shop iguana they had made their name on. Iguanas from the *Cyclura* genus were land lizards, living examples of *Jurassic Park*. Isolated on islands peppering the Caribbean, they were sometimes the largest animals on their islands, great stegosaurus-like beasts, highly speciated as a result of their isolation, and small in number because of the house cats and pigs man had brought with him to the islands.

Rileyi iguanas were too high profile, and his father's had no papers. How many strikes did his father think you got in life? With Ray's criminal record, did he think the government would look the other way?

Iguana people were nuts about their lizards. There were nonprofit organizations all over the world dedicated to preserving rare iguana species. The Bahamas had just celebrated the five hundredth anniversary of Christopher Columbus's landfall in America. To commemorate the occasion, they'd put Columbus's face on one side of the 1992 one-dollar bill and a *rileyi* iguana on the other. *Did*

Ray think the feds would not come after somebody who sold a fucking rileyi?

If Bepler got wind that they had even a single *rileyi,* Strictly Reptiles was dead. Ray listened to his son rant, and then he asked Cunningham to look for more. The compromise was that Ray had to keep his iguanas at home. Ray agreed, but when it got too cold he broke the agreement. He brought them in. One of the employees who packed shipments approached Ray. "Pops," he said, "would you mind if I took some photographs?"

"Sure," Ray said. Mike was not around. "Take one home if you want."

It was his birthday, December 19, 1993, when Mike and Michelle landed at JFK International Airport on their way home from Indonesia. They got off the plane and had passed through immigration when a U.S. Customs official said, "Happy Birthday," and directed them to stand aside. Van Nostrand looked around. Customs had a small army, maybe ten people, there to meet him. They let the entire airplane go by before signaling Van Nostrand forward. "Smuggler," someone muttered. Inspectors took away his and Michelle's luggage and began picking through their belongings. "What are you looking for?" he challenged. He hated it when people touched his things, although it was nice that Chip had remembered his birthday.

They found nothing.

The Bat Cave

Less than a year later, in November 1994, U.S. Interior Secretary Bruce Babbitt stood in the sparkling new Broward County Convention Center, in Fort Lauderdale, Florida, and welcomed delegates to the ninth biennial meeting of the United Nations Convention on International Trade in Endangered Species (CITES). With 124 members, CITES was the world's largest environmental treaty, and though it had been drafted in Washington, D.C., in 1973, this was the first time the parties involved had gathered in the United States since the treaty had entered into force.

A diplomatic host, Babbitt started his speech by praising CITES for its successes, particularly for what it had done for the African elephant. Prior to a CITES-imposed ban on ivory, poachers had shot an estimated 70,000 African elephants a year, one elephant every eight minutes.

After the species received CITES protection, elephant kills plummeted, from 2,000 a year in Kenya, for example, to less than 20. The leopard had prospered similarly. Before CITES, the United States alone had imported 7,000 leopard skins a year, mostly for coats. Now, Babbitt said, the U.S. market for leopard-skin coats had virtually disappeared. Trade in endangered tropical birds had also recently fallen as a result of CITES protections.

Finished with the good news, the secretary proceeded to the heart of his keynote address: law enforcement. The black market trade in wildlife, he said, had made a mockery of law enforcement. CITES would fail if the parties failed to enforce it.

The CITES meeting was big news, and the press was already well ahead of Babbitt in criticizing the world's efforts at law enforcement. *Time* had just published a story on the global influence of organized crime in the wildlife business. The article, "Animal Genocide, Mob Style," identified the world's key criminal hot spots: In Japan, yakuza were poaching protected whales for sushi. Russian mafia had cornered the infamous Moscow Bird Market, where in addition to puppies and birds from all over the world, a buyer could find protected chimpanzees, walrus ivory, and tiger-skin rugs.

Organized crime brought a new level of violence to the wildlife trade. When the Russian government went after a mob-connected wildlife smuggler, the mafia blew up the investigator's apartment, with his wife and child inside. In just two years, twenty-four Russian investigators had been killed on duty.

Embarrassingly, the American city *Time* highlighted in its exposé was the unofficial cohost to the CITES conference, Miami. South American drug cartels smuggling into Miami had recently shifted from hiding cocaine in cement utility poles to stuffing it inside polar bear skins and live boa constrictors with their anuses sewn closed. Tropical fish, perhaps the most unexamined import in the pet business, were coming in double-wrapped inside bags of what looked like water but was actually a layer of liquefied cocaine.

To Babbitt's further embarrassment, the South Florida press was alive with its own indictments. The *Miami Herald* called Miami "the Poachers' Playground." It said that illegal trade in endangered species was second only to the traffic in illegal drugs. The Fort Lauderdale *Sun-Sentinel* added that the most frequently smuggled wildlife coming through South Florida was reptiles.

Babbitt implored delegates from the 124 member countries to do something serious about wildlife crime. Ironically, given how close the conference center was to Strictly Reptiles' facility, he also wanted them to get out and enjoy the wonders of their South Florida environment. To encourage their sightseeing, he made National Park Service personnel available as tour guides. Delegates could travel Alligator Alley into the Everglades, they could visit the local beaches in Miami and Fort Lauderdale, they could take a trip to the Florida Keys National Marine Sanctuary or to Biscayne National Park. Along their travels, he said, they should take the time to talk with local people working together to solve natural resource issues. Delegates completed a survey to determine which of the local environmental attractions they wanted to see most.

On a hot Saturday afternoon, one week into their negotiations, delegates to the United Nations Convention on

International Trade in Endangered Species toppled out of
a tour bus and into the blazing South Florida sun. They
poured across a blacktop parking lot and into the air-
conditioned comfort of the Sawgrass Mills shopping mall,
bearing credit cards and cash. It turned out that what
CITES delegates really wanted to do was shop.

Shopping, of course, explained everything.

~~~~~

The ninety-eight Indian star tortoises entered the
United States bound for Strictly Reptiles two weeks before
the Fort Lauderdale CITES conference opened. According
to their paperwork, they'd been captive-bred in Dubai,
UAE.

Wildlife Inspector Mike Knowles reviewed the shipment. Everything about the tortoises and their paperwork
appeared to be in order. There were three wooden crates,
totaling 130 pounds. They had flown to Miami from Dubai
via Amsterdam, a relatively direct route. Still, they were
headed to Strictly Reptiles.

Knowles called Bepler.

After examining the paperwork, Bepler agreed that
CITES permit no. 01166 appeared authentic. It declared
that the tortoises had been born in captivity and supplied
by a company in Dubai called Abu Hanadi Ornaments
for Birds and Pets, a "breeder and farmer," according to
the company's letterhead. The permit had been stamped
and signed by the deputy minister of the UAE's Ministry
of Agriculture and Fisheries. Everything looked official.
Still, something smelled rotten. The UAE was notorious
for turning a blind eye toward CITES, making the country
a haven for illegal trade in all kinds of wildlife, including

rare snow leopards and hunting falcons, as well as products derived from endangered species, such as caviar and shahtoosh scarves.

Earlier in the year, the CITES secretariat in Geneva had sent out a notice alerting parties that four countries—Myanmar, Seychelles, Tanzania, and the UAE—were issuing fake captive-bred permits for Indian star tortoises. The response of the U.S. government to the warning had been less supportive than a wildlife officer like Bepler would have liked. The United States replied that if an exporting country said an animal was captive-bred, then the U.S. government was not going to question it. In fact, American CITES officials advised, the United States had already let in Indian star tortoises from the UAE.

Despite the fact that India and Pakistan both prohibited commercial export of star tortoises and Sri Lanka required a special permit—so that export of the species from its native range should theoretically be minute—tens of thousands of Indian star tortoises were sold around the world every year.

When Van Nostrand's older brother, Ray Jr., showed up to collect the star tortoise shipment, he was informed that the tortoises were being conditionally released to Strictly Reptiles pending investigation. He could take them, but Strictly Reptiles could not sell or dispose of them. Bepler kept nine to investigate.

"The Secretariat *strongly* recommends that the U.S. not accept the import," CITES enforcement officer John Gavitt wrote to Bepler's supervisor from Geneva. Sources indicated, he said, that star tortoises from the UAE were smuggled from India.

Bepler was now nose to nose with the dark side of CITES. Under the CITES permit system, it was not the animals that were valuable anymore; it was the paperwork. Given access to the right government official, men like Van Nostrand could turn a well-intentioned system into a laundromat.

Bepler flew the nine specimens to John Behler, the curator of reptiles at the Bronx Zoo, for an examination. Behler (who found his own name so similar to Bepler's in print that he spelled "Bepler" with two *p*'s) chaired the World Conservation Union's Tortoise and Freshwater Turtle Specialist Group. He was also a longtime friend of the Fish and Wildlife Service, having helped years ago with the Molt investigation. Within a week, Behler had issued a report to "Beppler" concluding that the star tortoises were not captive-bred. He estimated that they had been taken from the wild sometime within the past four months.

Further, Behler emphasized, the UAE had no known Indian star tortoise breeding facilities. Lest there be any doubt about what he was trying to say, Behler concluded his report with this line: "We firmly believe that the animals in question are a product of illegal take and urge that the tortoises in seizure not be released to commercial activity."

Mike Van Nostrand was not to be outdone. His father invited F. William "Bill" Zeigler, the curator of the Miami Metrozoo and an award-winning reptile expert, to inspect their remaining eighty-nine star tortoises. Zeigler wrote a letter giving his opinion, which he said was based on twenty years of seeing newly imported wild-caught tortoises. His assessment, he wrote, was "that the animals were captive bred."

On November 8, opening day of the CITES conference only a few miles away, Bepler informed Strictly Reptiles that he intended to seize the tortoises, citing violation of the Endangered Species Act.

Mike Van Nostrand erupted. He accused Bepler of selective enforcement. Had it been any other importer, he said, Fish and Wildlife would have let the tortoises through. In fact, he'd already heard that the wildlife inspector who'd first examined the shipment had thought everything looked good and had wanted to let it through. It was Bepler who'd stopped the shipment, and the only reason he'd done so was that he had it in for Van Nostrand personally. That was not law enforcement, that was vendetta.

Van Nostrand's lawyer, Patrick O'Brien, faxed an urgent letter to the UAE ambassador. The ambassador's office called O'Brien and suggested that he write to the country's minister of agriculture and fisheries, in Dubai.

Three days before the conclusion of the Fort Lauderdale CITES meeting, O'Brien got a response from Dubai confirming that the CITES permit was indeed genuine and that the Indian star tortoises had been captive-bred. The letter was signed by Dr. Ali A. Arab, director of the Animal Wealth Department, Ministry of Agriculture and Fisheries, CITES Management Authority of the UAE.

Suddenly Bepler found himself at odds with the very system he had committed his professional life to upholding. CITES was a system of rules. It was a framework for channeling commercial wildlife trade, stopping it only when necessary to save a species from extinction. That was the compromise inherent in the treaty. If you obeyed the rules, you got to buy and sell your wildlife.

And yet Bepler knew in his gut that Van Nostrand had smuggled the tortoises. The law made no provision for instinct. If he was wrong, and the star tortoises really had been captive-bred in Dubai, then it was not Van Nostrand who was flouting the CITES system to pursue his own agenda. It was Special Agent Charles R. Bepler Jr., the one who followed the rules, even ones that were not written down, like the "catch and release" principle he and his father had honored when he was a boy.

But if he was right and Van Nostrand had laundered the star tortoises through the UAE, then Michael Van Nostrand controlled a CITES party. With the UAE in his pocket, Van Nostrand could ship reptiles from anywhere in the world, and no matter how soiled with endangerment the species was, a captive-bred stamp from Dubai would launder it clean.

The UAE was not the only country blinking a warning to him. After Bepler stopped a shipment from Cameroon whose paperwork was so poorly doctored he could still read the name of the original recipient under the words "Strictly Reptiles," the government of Cameroon wrote to assure the Fish and Wildlife Service that Strictly Reptiles' permit was valid: "The typist made a typographical error while typing the document," wrote the director of the Department of Wildlife and Protected Areas. "She was forced to errace [sic] it." This letter, too, struck Bepler as suspect, since it had been faxed directly to Strictly Reptiles. He demanded that Van Nostrand apply for another permit, but got no response.

In a case involving protected lizards, Indonesian CITES authorities assured the U.S. government that Strictly Reptiles and its supplier Firma Hasco qualified for an exception to Indonesia's protection laws because of the scientific research on tree monitor lizards Strictly Reptiles was doing. As evidence it enclosed a letter from Michael Van Nostrand asking that Firma Hasco be given a CITES export permit so he could get new blood for the breeding project he had been conducting "for many years." Apparently enjoying the irony, Van Nostrand had added a line that was true: "It will be a great contribution to save our project from being cancelled or coming to a dead end."

Bepler looked into Strictly Reptiles' prior imports of Indian star tortoises. It turned out Van Nostrand had sourced star tortoises from the UAE before. Previously, however, those shipments had gone first to a man in Malaysia named Anson Wong. Bepler knew Wong's name. U.S. Fish and Wildlife considered him possibly the world's biggest illegal wildlife trafficker. Two years earlier, a question had been raised about a similar shipment of Indian star tortoises headed to Van Nostrand via Wong. In response, Penang's director of the Department of Wildlife and National Parks—the state's top CITES official—had written a letter to clear things up on behalf of Wong and Van Nostrand. That same government official was a Malaysian delegate to the CITES conference going on right across town.

On closing day of the Fort Lauderdale conference, as CITES attendees were buying T-shirts that read "Second Only to Drugs," Bepler seized the remaining eighty-nine Indian star tortoises from Strictly Reptiles.

Rules, he decided, had their limits.

~~~~~

Now Bepler had almost one hundred tortoises to care for. Van Nostrand filed papers claiming he should be allowed to care for the tortoises as a conditional release, but Bepler refused. Seizing animals was certainly no help to the animals themselves. All 347 tortoises he had seized from Medina were dead. The service was not good at keeping wildlife alive. Underfunding for investigative services was equaled by underfunding for the care of seized animals. Agents did not have elite refuges to take confiscated wildlife to, so they freelanced. Developing a network of public and private caretakers was part of the job, although finding a reptile keeper with no strings to Van Nostrand was difficult.

The Miami office had a caretaking contract with a young man who supplied wildlife for television commercials and films. The man's home was a living version of *Ace Ventura, Pet Detective*. He had a spider monkey on his couch, a lion in a backyard cage, rattlesnakes in tanks in a bedroom, macaws. The man did not consider tortoises good candidates for fashion advertising, but he accepted them anyway. He kept the tortoises in a plastic kiddie pool.

There was little Bepler could do. To protect wildlife, he had to stop Van Nostrand and stomach the unavoidable losses in the meantime. A recent experience had made that especially difficult. The DEA called the case Operation Cocaine Constrictor. A few months earlier a shipment of 312 live boa constrictors had arrived in Miami from Bogotá, Colombia. Customs inspectors, noticing a strange bulge inside one of the snakes, X-rayed it and discovered two condoms, each filled with four ounces of cocaine. The presence of narcotics gave the DEA authority over the investigation, and the DEA decided to do a controlled delivery, letting the shipment go through to see who picked it up. At one P.M., Bepler accompanied DEA agents in a stakeout of a van whose driver had retrieved the shipment at Miami International and had delivered it to an apartment complex north of Miami. The man got out of the van, went inside an apartment building, and disappeared.

In growing frustration, Bepler watched the van and the building while the boa constrictors sat inside the van all afternoon under the hot Florida sun, waiting for a pickup that never came. The next day, the DEA got a search warrant for the van. What Bepler saw when he entered the vehicle made him sick. Some two hundred adult boa constrictors were dead. The snakes had cooked and melted and mixed with spilled cocaine. Their intestinal tracts had dissolved, and many of the living were bleeding out at both ends, writhing in bags, and creating a horrible stew. Bepler waded into the blood and picked out the survivors. He sent them to Miami's Metrozoo, where they continued to die. In all, eighty pounds of cocaine had been hidden inside the snakes, whose anuses had been sewn shut.

Conservationists believe that once an animal is removed from the wild it is "biologically dead," which is to say, it is no longer part of an ecosystem. But that was not how Bepler felt. For reasons that went back to his childhood, Bepler could not get over that scene, the death and the waste. He had nightmares about it.

It took nothing to bring the image back to him—he'd open the evidence refrigerator hard enough to cause a breeze, or pick up an old box of raw coral, and the memory of the dead snakes would return to him out of nowhere. All at once he would be there, in the van with the blood and the heat, and over and over he vowed that death like that would not happen again on his watch.

And so when it came to keeping the animals alive,

he knew Van Nostrand was probably a better temporary steward than the service, but he couldn't let Van Nostrand get control of them. The case against Strictly Reptiles depended on a showing that the star tortoises had been wild-caught. Give Van Nostrand the slightest opportunity and, Bepler knew, he would turn it into more cash.

Bepler stood up from his desk. He could not think sitting down. He needed to move. Robin laughed about it sometimes, about how he walked out his thoughts, pacing in a circle, always tapping his fingers against a thigh. Some things he could not stomach, would not stomach.

~~~~~

Bepler walked into his supervisor's office and shut the door. Miami was the largest single importer of exotic animals in the world. Fighting the illegal commercialization of endangered wildlife was their number one priority. *What the hell were they doing?* The CITES conference had been an embarrassment. While bureaucrats argued population theory and went shopping, Fish and Wildlife had just gone head to head with Van Nostrand and Anson Wong, the "law enforcement problem" everybody at the conference had really been talking about. The Miami office might not have lost, but seizing ninety-eight tortoises was no victory either.

As far as Bepler could tell, Van Nostrand's breeder in Dubai did not exist. Abu Hanadi Ornaments' CITES permit listed only a post office box, so Bepler had demanded that Van Nostrand provide the breeder's actual location. Van Nostrand complied through his lawyer. When investigators checked the address, they found a flower shop.

Every other smuggler they grabbed at Miami International and every informant who told them anything gave them a Strictly Reptiles story. It was coming on three years since Medina, and they had been able to do nothing about Van Nostrand. Less than nothing. Had word gotten around? Had they had that chilling effect on crime that they always talked about? The smugglers were still coming. A year before Bepler had arrested an Argentine man entering Miami International Airport with the exact same M.O. as Medina's. Lucio Coronel got off a plane from Buenos Aires on a Sunday morning wheeling a big, hard-sided suitcase up to the customs line. Ceramics, he said he was carrying. The X-ray showed skeletons. Inside his suitcase, Coronel carried 107 chaco tortoises, 103 red-footed tortoises, 76 tartaruga turtles, 5 Argentine boa constrictors, 7 rainbow boas, 7 parrot snakes, 20 tarantulas, 10 scorpions, 90 tree frogs, 20 red tegu lizards, a dozen or so other lizards, and 2 South American rattlesnakes. All in one suitcase! He was donating them to the Bronx Zoo, he told Bepler.

Thanks to Chris McAliley's Environmental Crimes Section, Coronel was sentenced to fifteen months in prison. But catching one low-level smuggler was like seeing one cockroach in your kitchen: there were plenty more out there. By the time Coronel settled into prison there would be somebody else wheeling in a suitcase from Argentina. Argentina was minor. A suitcase from Argentina was *the easy case*.

How many times had they gone into Strictly Reptiles themselves? Mike Van Nostrand sitting there at his desk, grave as a mortician, handing over the documents they requested, apologizing that others did not exist. All the while, at the edges of those green eyes, was that sparkle. He was laughing. Laughing at *them*!

More proof? Bepler had it lying on his desk. *Reptiles,* the number one magazine in the reptile hobby, had just done an in-depth story on endangered Caribbean iguanas. The species they put on the cover was a gorgeous *Cyclura rileyi cristata,* the Sandy Cay rock iguana. According to the article, fewer then five hundred animals were known to exist in the wild, but you could open up the magazine and find the exact location for one of them. The photographer worked at Strictly Reptiles.

Bepler's supervisor, Jorge Picon, nodded. He knew. They all knew. Strictly Reptiles was an international import-export company with clients in virtually every country in the world. Any imported reptile in any pet shop in the United States had a decent chance of being a Strictly Reptiles–sourced animal. It was a multimillion-dollar operation, and that was just the legal side.

But what was Picon supposed to do? To get Mike Van Nostrand on criminal charges, they had to prove he *knew* the animals he was buying were illegal. This wasn't like prosecuting drug trafficking. With cocaine, all you had to do was see a bag of white powder on a man's desk to arrest him; but catch a man with an endangered tortoise on his desk and that was not the end—that was the beginning. That was the *easy* part. Because with animals you had to prove that the man with the endangered species on his desk *knew* it had been smuggled illegally. And every smuggler had memorized exactly what to say: He told me it was captive-bred.

To prove that Van Nostrand *knew* about these smugglers, they had to find a weak spot in his network. That took resources Picon did not have. The Miami Division had just three special agents to cover all of South Florida, the Keys, Puerto Rico, and the U.S. Virgin Islands *combined*. That meant three agents to investigate every illegal plant or animal that came through the port of Miami, by plane or by boat. It meant three agents to police the waterways against manatee abusers. Three agents to wade into the marshes before dawn to await duck poachers and Key deer hunters and dove baiters. Three agents to watch over the Florida panther, three to stop Mexican restaurants from serving up sea turtle eggs, three to force beachside hotels to dim their lights so that the sea turtles that did hatch could follow the reflected light of the moon to the Atlantic Ocean instead of finding death in the artificial illumination of a well-lit parking lot.

There were only 205 Fish and Wildlife special agents *in the whole country*. The Division of Law Enforcement was broken down into seven regional offices. Going after one particular criminal or group of criminals in any concerted way meant that others would go free. When Region 2 investigated a million-dollar business trading in illegal bobcat pelts, poachers of canvasback and redhead ducks on Ute Lake in New Mexico and the Texas coast went free. When Region 6, home to a block of eight states from Kansas to Montana, focused on waterfowl poachers, they could do nothing about the canned cougar hunting and bobcat smuggling going on in those states.

Miami was part of Region 4, headquartered in Atlanta. Region 4 covered all states east of Texas and south of North Carolina, plus, of course, the Keys, the U.S. Virgin Islands, and Puerto Rico. Region 4 was considered the most understaffed regional office in the country. Atlanta had just spent two years on a special task force devoted to poaching of migratory waterfowl centered in Louisiana. The operation was considered successful, but not by everyone. It had required eight special agents from outside Louisiana and had crippled enforcement throughout the region. Dozens of wildlife crimes in Alabama, Arkansas, and Mississippi had gone completely unaddressed.

Every year Region 4 ran out of money. Every year field agents came in out of the marshes and sat deskbound for as many as five months, waiting for another fiscal year to come around, like deer hunters waiting for fall. Every region had its own version of the story. It was not just the lack of up-front manpower Picon had to think about; the back end took resources, too. To close a major deer-and-elk-poaching operation in Colorado's San Luis Valley, the service had sent one man undercover for two and a half years, and when he came out with evidence on fifty poachers, it took 275 agents from the Fish and Wildlife Service and other federal and state enforcement agencies to make the arrests and seizures.

Picon had three special agents, including Bepler, plus five wildlife inspectors. As in New York, you did not have to look hard for cases. They got a minimum of 300 shipments of tropical fish in per week, 100 to 200 boxes per shipment—all five of Picon's inspectors could work twenty-four hours a day and still never find all the liquid cocaine coming in. Not that they would ever get the authority to handle a narcotics case anyway—that was the DEA's turf.

Smugglers were sewing snakes into their clothes, hiding marmosets in their pockets. They hid animals in their socks, in their cleavage, in the crotches of their jeans. They painted cockatoo eggs and brought them in as Easter baskets; they stuffed tortoises into giant teddy bears. They painted the feathers on gold-capped conures green. They dyed orangutans black. Inspectors found cobras loose in some shipments. Best, and most simple of all, smugglers were paying off government officials—no doubt some of the officials who had just left the CITES convention.

South American drug cartels had begun smuggling in wildlife for its own sake—the profit margins were just as high as those on cocaine, and the penalties were almost nonexistent. Over and over they faced that reality. Picon could rattle off their situation in his sleep: Miami was number one in U.S. live wildlife imports, and number one in both drug and wildlife smuggling. He had five inspectors to examine over 14,000 shipments per year. His inspection rate was the lowest in the country...

Bepler knew the difficulties the office faced, probably better than Picon. He was an investigator, and his wife was an inspector—between them, they saw it all. He and Robin were still unpacking boxes of their own, hardly settled into their new home a week, when Robin had an opportunity to inspect a Strictly Reptiles shipment firsthand: seventy-two monitor lizards, seventy of them dead. That was the price of commercialized wildlife: death was treated as an "acceptable loss," no different from rotten fruit. It was unavoidable, bad enough on its own, but Van Nostrand was a criminal.

Robin had quickly been promoted to supervisor for Miami. She had done what she could to get inspections on track, but the two of them had decided there were other things in life that were important, too. Recently, Robin had left the service to have their first child, a son.

Bepler knew what Robin had faced as head wildlife inspector, and he knew what he faced as the Miami office's de facto special agent for reptile smuggling. Medina had gotten him here. *The easy case.* Sure, he'd turned Medina, persuaded him to plead guilty and admit his smuggling was for Strictly. But he'd gotten nowhere that mattered. If he had the Medina arrest to do over again, he would do a controlled delivery. Anyone would. But they had invited *America's Most Wanted* to the airport that day, believing that some positive publicity might help balance the scales a little for their underfinanced and understaffed office. It was to be a training bust, after all. But then Medina had linked them to Strictly Reptiles... Hell, Fish and Wildlife had even gotten clever and sued Van Nostrand for $613,000, a crippling sum for most reptile dealers. Instead of caving in, Van Nostrand had hired those lawyers that were beating them up over the Indian star tortoises, as well as a dozen other species.

To get Van Nostrand they had to find a way to get out in front of him. Turning mules into informants was *reactive*. Miami had already sent a memo to that effect over to the regional office in Atlanta. As far as Bepler knew, the memo had been filed under a log. He couldn't blame them. If you were going to stick your neck out on a new investigation, you wanted to do it over a resource that was going to get you positive attention and more funding. Reptiles were hardly that.

If they were going to stop Van Nostrand, they had to prove criminal intent, and they were going to have to get that proof on their own.

Bepler told Picon what he had in mind.

Jorge Picon had transferred down from headquarters, but he was no conventional suit. He had just authorized what had become the most famous sting in U.S. Fish and Wildlife history. Some Mexican zoo officials wanted to buy a gorilla, so Terry English dressed up in a gorilla suit and sat in a cage while Picon, pretending to be a corrupt zoo official, sold him. The cage was set up in the hold of a DC-3 aircraft, ready to fly the smugglers and their gorilla to Mexico. Agents had scattered gorilla dung on the tarmac outside and piled it inside the cage to give the plane a wild animal smell. When the lead buyer got too close to the cage, English slammed an angry shoulder into the door. Then he returned to a dark corner and grunted. The sting worked so well that one defendant nearly had a heart attack when English opened the cage door and jumped on him. Minutes later English took his gorilla head off and had a cigarette.

Picon listened as Bepler sketched out his idea. He liked Bepler's plan, but after considering what it entailed, he said it was not his decision to make. Picon called his other two special agents, Jennifer English and Eddie McKissick, into his office. (After a split with Jennifer, Terry English had transferred to South Carolina.)

The Miami Division of Law Enforcement operated out of a single office unit in the back of the Doral West industrial complex, not far from Miami International Airport. It was a tiny facility, designed more like a loft apartment for college newlyweds than a federal headquarters for fighting international wildlife crime. The first floor had only a

small reception desk and a storage room for refrigerating
dead animals and maintaining other evidence. The second
floor consisted of a couple of cubicles for agents and two
cramped offices.

Picon's office was too small to seat all three of his special agents at one time. They stood while Picon breathed
in over his mustache. "Chip has a proposal," he said.

Bepler made his pitch. Law Enforcement was supposed to be the predator's predator, and yet all they did
was hand Mike Van Nostrand a *ticket,* a civil fine hardly
more substantial than a parking ticket. Even when they
knew they were right they often had to "conditionally
release" smuggled animals back to Strictly Reptiles pending further investigation. Did it work? Van Nostrand had
just bought a beautiful thirty-two-foot Luhrs fishing boat;
the name emblazoned on the boat's stern was *Conditional
Release*!

For Bepler the question was simple. The motivation
for depleting wildlife was greed, the same motive at the
bottom of every other form of organized crime. Catching
mules and stopping couriers might get publicity, but in the
end couriers were nothing more than grocery clerks sent
by Mike Van Nostrand. Strictly Reptiles was a factory.

The Fish and Wildlife Service could have all the display
booths with poached rhino heads and tiger-skin rugs at all
the CITES meetings until the end of time, but if they could
not stop Strictly Reptiles, they should not even be in the
wildlife-protection business. Although he did not say it
directly, he had already made up his mind. If they would
not attack the engine, then there was no point to his working wildlife anymore. If they would not commit to taking
down Strictly Reptiles, he would quit the service.

"I want to work exclusively on Strictly Reptiles," Bepler said.

In a three-agent office, that meant his colleagues would have to work much, much longer hours. English looked at her friend. Chip had settled in during the three years since they had arrested Tomas Medina together. He had a mouth on him. He would get wound up over some scumbag, as he referred to criminals, and let his New York side loose. Once in a while somebody would have to rein him in. "Chip," they would say, "Mrs. Medina." Chip would look up at their secretary—no relation to the smuggler—and grimace: "Aw, I'm fucking sorry, Mrs. Medina." And he would realize he had done it again. And they would all laugh together.

Jennifer English had been putting up with Strictly Reptiles for years, watching Mike Van Nostrand grow more powerful as her office struggled to keep pace. It was not just reptiles; he was hiding hedgehogs inside crates marked "Nile monitors." Genets—catlike mammals—he imported came in near death.

Picon had recently hired a new special agent. They called themselves the Mod Squad. English was Julie, Bepler was Pete, and the newest guy, Eddie McKissick, was Linc. McKissick had been introduced to Mike Van Nostrand already. Not long after his transfer to Miami, a Strictly Reptiles shipment had been McKissick's *easy case*.

The shipment had come in from Egypt at a time when Egypt was officially closed to all wildlife trade. An export ban—it really could not be easier, and given Strictly Reptiles' reputation, McKissick was proud as hell to get such an easy shot at Van Nostrand. And then the letters came. Egypt's undersecretary of state for zoos and the

Egyptian Wildlife Service wrote that Strictly Reptiles had been granted an exception to his country's export ban. A follow-up letter arrived from the Egyptian embassy in Washington, D.C., supporting Strictly Reptiles.

McKissick seized the animals anyway, and that same day got a faxed letter from the director general of Egypt's wildlife service confirming his government's approval of an exception for Strictly Reptiles. The seizure was deemed inappropriate and McKissick was required to personally return the animals to Van Nostrand. Worst of all, almost two hundred of the lizards he brought back were dead.

Van Nostrand was loud and profane. He once yelled so violently at Jennifer English—telling her this was his business, his "shop"—that McKissick picked up a camera he knew had no film in it and began snapping photos around the facility. It got Van Nostrand to turn from his quarry, which was all both agents wanted—to get out of the building with some balance left in their relationship.

So yes, for his personality alone, McKissick and English agreed, they wanted Van Nostrand gone. And as wildlife officers, it was their responsibility to stop any reptile smuggler. But the implications of arresting Van Nostrand ran to far more than just reptile smuggling. McKissick saw the bigger picture: they were getting beaten so badly, there was no reason for any animal importer to obey the law. Strictly Reptiles was a coal-mine canary for the illegal wildlife business not only in South Florida but around the world. As long as Strictly was getting away with smuggling, everyone else, big or small, dealing in plants or animals, knew that they, too, had a chance.

To restore order to the entire animal kingdom, they had to go after Mike Van Nostrand, and they had to put him in jail. Even better, they would shut Strictly Reptiles down for good. Picon himself said he would take a pull at the duty roster. And so the entire Miami office formed a pact. They would get Mike Van Nostrand, and they would close him down.

In prosecutorial terms, what they were launching was an "impact case," a case whose implications were far-reaching for the American public. In health care and product liability, tobacco suits were impact cases. In the exotic-animal world, Strictly Reptiles would be their impact case—one way or the other.

They were betting far more than the reptile world on their choice. Limited funding for their office meant that they were staking the lives of every plant and animal in their jurisdiction—Key deer, manatees, Florida panthers, birds, fish, imported species, everything—on catching Van Nostrand. Bepler would be betting his career. The easy case had turned into the case that would define his professional life, for good or for bad.

He cleared out his desk and carried his things down-stairs to the storage room. There, opposite the dead speci-mens' refrigerator, he set up his command center. There would be no telephone. No outside light. The storage room was twice the size of Picon's office upstairs. His colleagues dubbed it the Bat Cave.

Cat and Mouse

V an Nostrand settled into his new location. His new ten-thousand-square-foot warehouse in Hollywood, Florida, was surrounded by a chain-link fence topped with barbed wire. For reasons he kept to himself, he sealed off the entrance gate Frito-Lay had used and cut open another one on the opposite side of the property. One effect of the change was that because the building sat strangely deep in the pocket of its lot, all comings and goings were now concealed from the street.

He decorated his office in a style befitting a porn executive: faux-snakeskin walls, a zebra-skin throw. He installed dark one-way mirrors for keeping an eye on his employees and he set up a corner fish tank; in it he kept a pair of Fly River turtles that he had smuggled in from Andre Van Meer in Indonesia. Named for New Guinea's Fly River, they have a skin-covered shell, a piglike snout, and are the world's only freshwater turtle with flippers. Coincidentally, they do seem to fly as they move through water, like a sea turtle. Considered a national treasure, the species was strictly protected throughout its range. No exports were allowed for the pet trade. He and Van Meer had smuggled these as part of their new operation. Van Nostrand had them on his price list for $1,000 apiece, and they were selling well.

In the administrative office for his clerical staff he added desks for his father and his older brother. Clocks on the wall gave the time in Los Angeles, Germany, Hong Kong, and Hollywood, Florida. He installed closed-circuit cameras throughout the building.

Instead of a Mercedes or a Cadillac, either of which he could easily afford now, he drove to work in a monstrous off-road Ford 4x4 set on thirty-eight-inch Super Swamper tires, the truck jacked up so high off the ground he had trouble climbing into it. It cost more than most luxury cars. At traffic lights, he sat rumbling and shaking above the rest of the world, music blaring, while teenage boys looked up at him with envy in their eyes and their parents turned away.

"If we lose that," Agent McKissick told Bepler during one of their rolling surveillances, "we both need to go back to police training."

There was no way they could lose Van Nostrand. He was growing physically larger by the day, and wherever he went he bellowed, that terrible and profane mouth consuming the silence around him, turning heads.

He knew Bepler was after him. He'd heard from other importers that Bepler was asking about him, leaning on people to give him dirt on Strictly. "Let him come," he thought. "Cat and mouse. Mano a mano." As Van Nostrand's mother had told him one time, these were not your A and B students in law enforcement, these were your C and D students, no better than you at all. To that analysis he'd added his own: these were biology majors he was dealing with in U.S. Fish and Wildlife, not FBI-trained investigators.

Inside his warehouse, he housed most lizards and tortoises by species in cattle feed tubs set inside waist-high wooden cabinets, running the length of the building. He kept aquatic turtles and crocodilians in great plastic tubs with independent plumbing. Climbing lizards and expensive chameleons were put in coat-closet-sized screen cages that could be wheeled out onto the loading dock to get sun. He built a frog room, an arachnid room, two python rooms (one for young and small species, and another for large adults), a room for colubrids (harmless species common to the U.S. and Asia), and a locked, venomous room. Outside the administrative office was an area for packing and unloading shipments.

He installed two industrial walk-in freezers. He used them to store dead animals. Santeria practitioners came in to buy dead snakes and spiders for their voodoo rituals. There was no way for Bepler to tell whether a dead tortoise had been conditionally released two weeks ago or had died four years back. If the government came in to reclaim conditionally released animals, Van Nostrand first checked what he had in the freezer. Anything in there, he handed to Bepler.

One freezer was set at a higher temperature, more like a refrigerator. When the Department of Agriculture arrived to inspect his turtles, he could see them coming on the monitors from his outside cameras. He'd call out "Code Blue" on the factory intercom, and everybody knew which turtles to grab and stick in the refrigerator until the inspection was over.

His mules began to organize. They evolved from opportunists stuffing something in their pockets to professionals structuring their lives around the sure thing that was Strictly Reptiles. Dwayne Cunningham, the comedian, hopped the wall around the zoo on St. Martin for some really nice red-footed tortoises. He brought them home not to sell to Mike but to breed in his backyard, so that he could sell Van Nostrand the offspring. Fruit of the poisonous tree, sure, but Cunningham thought of himself as a curator, not a smuggler. He and his wife set up a reptile company, Cunningherps. Van Nostrand bought what they produced.

Van Nostrand giggled in awe over Phil Langston, a good ol' Georgia giant so physically dominating even Mike felt uncomfortable in his presence. Langston flew down to Nicaragua, where CITES quotas were small, and started pulling out red-eyed tree frogs by the hundreds. He would call up every three weeks or so and Van Nostrand would meet him at the shop after hours.

Nicaragua worked so well that Langston set up a "breeding farm" in Peru to give the appearance of captive-breeding reptiles while he poached Central and South American creatures straight out of a Dr. Seuss book: mata mata turtles, white-lipped mud turtles, red-cheeked mud turtles, sidenecks and twistnecks, and toad-headed turtles, to name just the turtle species. After that he flew to Haiti and smuggled in protected rhinoceros iguanas, packed literally like sardines into two suitcases, and Haitian ground boas, and tree boas, and dwarf boas . . .

There were never-proven rumors that Langston was CIA. Some kind of dropout rebel with the connections of a drug runner. Langston said all he did was pay some people working for the airlines.

Langston smuggled in what was probably Van Nostrand's favorite reptile: the caiman lizard from Peru. Half monitor lizard, half alligator, the caiman lizard has a knobby, armored back and flattened tail like an alligator, as well as the long, forked tongue of a monitor lizard. Its head is a colorful yellow or red, and its teeth include unusually flat molars for eating its primary food—snails. Van Nostrand sold hundreds of caiman lizards.

Anytime Mike's older brother, Ray Jr., saw Langston, his stomach sank. Junior had even less interest in reptiles than Mike did, and yet, among the Van Nostrand men, Junior most wanted the family reptile business to travel its course. His main job revolved around the airport— picking up and delivering shipments. In that way he was the family's first line of defense. He was the one standing with inspectors as they looked over his company's paperwork or crowbarred open a shipping crate. He was the one who had to pretend he was just as surprised as anyone else when a shipment his brother had ordered contained questionable animals. Junior didn't like any of it. A smuggler like Phil Langston would walk into the front office carrying a suitcase packed with caiman lizards and Junior would shake his head and walk out of the room. He was not aggressive like his younger brother, but he was fierce in his desire to protect the family. There was no need for Mike to constantly head their lives into a storm.

For Mike, it was fun. The money. The sneaking around. Men dominate the reptile industry, but they do not own it entirely. The same is true of reptile smuggling. Wives sewed bedsheets into tortoise carriers for their husbands to use as Medina had; others sewed secret pockets into their own dresses for trips between the United States and Europe. Germans walked into Strictly Reptiles wearing bird-watching vests, their pockets stuffed with frogs and turtles. So many smugglers were coming, Van Nostrand nicknamed the Comfort Inn up the road the Smugglers' Inn.

Smugglers quit his competitors to bring animals to him. A pair of Germans named Wolfgang Kloe and Frank Lehmeyer, tired of how slow Crutchfield was to pay them, began supplying Van Nostrand with illegal reptiles from Madagascar. The pair bought up endangered species such as radiated tortoises and Madagascar tree boas, traveling to nearby Réunion, the French-owned island, which put them back in the embrace of the European Union. From Réunion they flew home to Germany and then suitcased reptiles to Florida.

"I can't believe how stupid all these guys are, bringing this stuff in," Van Nostrand marveled to his lawyer one day.

"No, Michael," O'Brien replied. "It's not How stupid are they? It's How stupid are you? You're the one taking the animals. You have all these people coming in, and one of these days they won't be coming in for no reason. It will be a controlled delivery. The guy is going to be wired, he's going to offer you animals dusted with fluorescent powder..." O'Brien was impressed with Van Nostrand's ability to talk his way over any agent who came in his door; still, as an ex-agent himself, the lawyer knew that if you beat the government ten times, the eleventh time you're dead.

Smuggling accounted for only a fraction of Van Nostrand's total business. He was selling hundreds of thousands of legal pet-shop species every year—common green iguanas, red-legged tarantulas, boa constrictors, turtles. Taking a weekly price list at random from the period, Van Nostrand offered hermit crabs; a 5-foot-long caiman; 2 species of salamanders; 24 types of frogs; 22 tarantula species; 4 scorpion species; Florida centipedes; 83 lizard species (from geckos to the crocodile monitor); 22 boa species; 15 python species; 9 tortoise species; 20 different types of turtles (including smuggled Fly River turtles listed as "captive raised"); and 30 species of venomous snakes, including baby water moccasins for $5, baby red spitting cobras for $100, and a black mamba for $500. Venomous beaded lizards were $1,000 each. He listed three types of mammals for sale that week: fat-tail jirds (a gerbil), hedgehogs, and sugar gliders. The most expensive item on the list was a pair of giant Aldabra tortoises, a species rivaling the Galápagos tortoise as the world's largest, priced at $22,500 for the pair. Every Thursday, he faxed a new, updated price list to his customers.

He floated on top of a decade of new money flooding into the industry after the albino Burmese python was featured in *National Geographic,* but that money was now going up even faster because of a new approach to pythons: "designer breeding."

Because snakes have very few things that can go wrong with them (they're really just a hose with a mouth and two eyes), after the albino craze, entrepreneurs began "line breeding" pythons and other species at dramatic rates, inbreeding offspring to their parents, siblings to siblings, panning for genetic deviations in their snakes' colors and patterns. Often the most valuable gene was a "not-gene"— an axanthic ("not-yellow") gene, for example, which could be used to erase the yellow from a snake's skin. Breeding brown to albino gave you yellow; breeding yellow to axanthic gave you white. Stripes could be added or taken away. Line breeding itself unlocked genes that sometimes caused incredible things to "pop." Designers turned spotted brown snakes into orange snakes with lavender stripes. They turned sand-colored lizards fire red. Reptiles had become paint kits. Breeders called what they did "living art," and they gave their concoctions hot-rod names like Super Pastel Jungle, Albino Licorice Stick, Blazing Blizzard, and Dreamsicle.

All across the country, in convention centers, armories, hotel conference rooms, and high school gymnasiums, reptile shows were taking place. One species dominated the designer trend: the African ball python. The ball python was considered the perfect-sized snake for a pet; as a genetic canvas, fat enough to show color, it was the most valuable reptile in the world. African ball pythons were being sold in acrylic jewelry cases laid out on black felt—like diamond necklaces. Prices for genetically cultivated "designer pythons" were skyrocketing. The $30 retail ball python was seeing its designer price climb to $15,000, then $45,000, then $85,000. One breeder even paid $145,000 for a "completely white" ball python. And that was just one species. People were breeding designer lizards, albino turtles, and rare frogs.

A new industry had developed to house investment-grade ball pythons in gigantic "rack systems" that resembled library card catalogs six feet tall with plastic drawers the size of safe-deposit boxes. In the wild, ball pythons are sedentary, spending time hidden in rodent burrows. This tendency toward inactivity made them storable. Heat-controlled rack systems of twenty units or more amounted to hardware-store cabinets where instead of lock washers and wing nuts, each drawer contained genes. You opened a drawer, took out your "amelanistic" gene, dropped it into "genetic stripe" and *voilà*.

As an importer, Van Nostrand held a key to fresh design possibilities. He brought in forty thousand or so ball pythons a year, which he wholesaled to pet stores in lots of twenty-five for $16.50. Designer breeders begged Mike to call them whenever he saw something odd in his African shipments. Some paid him a fee just to have first look. They searched his imports for aberrations. Holding them under a desk lamp, they studied odd snakes, scale by scale, looking for signs that recessive genes might be locked inside them: mustaching around the lips of pythons, yellow along their bellies, signals breeders had identified as markers for hidden color or pattern traits. Traits that, after a few generations of line breeding, might appear as a popular new color or pattern.

Van Nostrand was making so much money he even missed opportunities—including one in particular. It happened at the National Reptile Breeders' Expo, the industry's annual trade-show bonanza. Started in Orlando, and later moved to Daytona Beach, the National Reptile Breeders' Expo was the Detroit Auto Show of the reptile world, the largest two-day reptile event in the world, where everyone from high-end designer breeders to the suppliers of Petco and Petsmart came to trade. For one weekend every

August, the best hotels along the ocean in Daytona Beach would be booked solid; across the street, the 85,000-square-foot Ocean Center would fill to the brim with reptile dealers and buyers from around the world: robed Japanese; millionaire Africans dressed like third-world dictators (when it came to the ball python, they were); Chinese, Germans, Koreans. And most of all, Americans. Rivaled only by the one-day Terraristika Hamm show in Hamm, Germany, the American expo was meant for business. It attracted, by necessity, smugglers from around the world, too. Every year, Strictly Reptiles had the expo's largest booth, often in the prime location near the door. In contrast to the jewelry storefronts of designer breeders and the jungle designs of some reptile specialists, Strictly Reptiles set up its display with reptiles housed in stacks of cheap cake tubs and deli cups from a party plastics store.

Van Nostrand knew everybody in the business, so when a tall, pale-eyed stranger introduced himself and asked a simple question, Mike yelled something rude at him and turned his back, not realizing how much outside money the reptile business had recently attracted.

The man was Karl Hart. Hart had far more money than Van Nostrand ever would, and he planned to use it to make his mark in the reptile industry. He had just opened an exotic-animal business in San Francisco he called Pac-Rim. Hart was interested in doing business with Van Nostrand, but if that wasn't going to work, he could compete against him instead.

Van Nostrand's frilled dragon operation was going very well. Andre Van Meer used three routes to smuggle him wild-caught frilled dragons. Van Meer shipped directly to Van Nostrand using "captive-bred" paperwork; he shipped to Van Nostrand via Anson Wong; and he shipped via his hometown, Breda, Holland.

Frilled dragons were protected under Indonesian and Australian domestic laws, but they were not listed with CITES, so Europe did not protect them. That made Europe a laundering opportunity.

Van Nostrand's goal was to corner the world market in frilled dragons. After the first few shipments, they were no longer especially valuable—he bought them for $125 and sold them for $250—but he was bringing in hundreds. It was exciting. Having odd species was part of what made his reputation: Strictly Reptiles was a one-stop reptile shop.

He was moving reptiles around the world, kiting and churning CITES documents. To keep Bepler off balance, he did not bring everything in through Miami. A wildlife inspector in Tampa was known to be afraid of snakes, so some shipments came in there. He routed shipments through New York, too.

Van Nostrand was into his best year ever, on track to make half a million tax-free smuggling dollars to go along with almost $8 million in declared sales. He planned to buy an even bigger boat. He already had the name picked out: *Pillage and Plunder.*

"You better get ready," he told Michelle, "because one of these days I'm going to jail." He would not concede that Bepler would get him, though it seemed that every time he did something, Bepler was there. Rather, he'd begun to sense that he was driving forward so rapidly that his momentum might take him beyond even his own control, as if prison was a place he *wanted* to go to. He was like a gas with no beaker to hold him. He expanded out almost to the point of losing himself, in a kind of frenzy for the rush that smuggling gave him, all the richer because someone was after him. He had always broken rules and he had never really been disciplined. He'd grown up in a never-never land of his father's making, with all the toys and guns and drugs and reptiles pirate dreams were made of. And what could Michelle do but watch? She had married him because he had a strong personality, the opposite of hers in many ways. There was no way to stop him.

~~~~~

Bepler would drift off sometimes, and Robin would let him go, knowing he would be back in a moment. He did not let his work push its way into their lives. Once in a while she would see him standing there and she would know to give him a moment to process whatever it was. They had their son, Robbie, named for Chip's father, who went by his middle name. They had their lives together.

Bepler walked his circle, thinking, tapping his slender index finger against his thigh. Van Nostrand was vacuuming the jungles only a few miles away, while he, the man who loved to be outdoors, spent his days in a windowless room, listening to the Marlins on a portable radio, pacing in circles.

He had a web of informants now. One had worked at Strictly Reptiles smuggling African tortoises and alligators, before opening his own reptile store. Others would drop in at Strictly to see something Van Nostrand had or to hear him talking, and then call Bepler. Informants had all sorts of motives for what they did. They wanted revenge or attention. Often they were a Van Nostrand competitor in search of an edge. That was something about the reptile industry: dealers informed on one another for competitive advantage. Price was one way to compete, but sending your competitor to jail or getting him a fine was another. Some reptile smugglers went to prison never knowing what their friends had done to them; others shrugged it off and returned to being friends again.

Bepler walked into Strictly Reptiles. He made a routine inspection of the new facility, noting the arachnid room and the frog room and the smell of paint still heavy in the air from a small football field of cages Van Nostrand had installed. He paused over a shipment of lizards he had argued with Van Nostrand about already—the dispute concerned exactly which species they were and whether they were permitted—and returned to Van Nostrand. "I'm seizing those lizards," he said.

"You can't have them," Van Nostrand replied, "because you're wrong."

"I'm taking them."

"No, you're not."

"Yes, I am."

"You're not. Try."

Bepler had brought a wildlife inspector with him. He directed the inspector to bag up the lizards. "Don't let him do it," Van Nostrand told his employee. A tug-of-war began between the two men. Van Nostrand dialed 911.

Officially, Strictly Reptiles was located in Hollywood, but it physically sat on the line between the towns of Hollywood and Davie. By closing the entrance on one side of his property and opening it on the other, Van Nostrand had shifted police jurisdiction for the warehouse from Hollywood to Davie. He'd grown up in Davie. He knew the Davie cops.

A squad car pulled into the Strictly Reptiles parking lot.

"You can't come in here and seize this man's inventory without the proper documentation," the Davie police officer said.

"Look," Bepler said, "I was in there. I saw the illegal evidence, and I am going to take it."

The officer shook his head. "If you told me it was cocaine or pot or drugs I would tend to agree with you, but those are live animals. You're saying those are illegal. I don't know that. You're really gonna have to get a search warrant if you want to take those animals from him..."

Then the officer called Van Nostrand outside. "Look, I'm not going to let him take your animals, but I'm telling you right now you need to clear this up because he's going to get a fucking search warrant and take your shit. So I would try to work this out."

The next day Bepler returned with a search warrant and seized the animals.

On another occasion, Van Nostrand shouted, "You're a fucking pussy!" at Bepler and slammed down the telephone. The next morning, Bepler showed up, search warrant in hand, and seized the animals, forcing Van Nostrand to shell out over thirty grand because he could not control his mouth.

Soon vines began to lace their way up the chain-link fence behind Van Nostrand's new building. Weeds grew along the former back gate. Bepler pulled up in the shadows of the old gate in his government-issued green Bronco and watched, taking down license-plate numbers, recording the faces of customers in his mind. Helpless.

~~~~~~

It began as an extra look at odd contraband: colorful frogs smuggled into Breda from South America. They were green and black poison arrow frogs, *Dendrobates auratus,* harmless once removed from their native diet and local environment. Beautiful, yes, but odd, thought the Netherlands customs authorities. How much could a little rubbery dot of color be worth? Enough, it turned out. A small team of investigators was formed, drawn from the Netherlands National Police; the Ministry of Justice; and the Netherlands Ministry of Agriculture, Nature Conservation, and Fisheries. It was led by Henry Ligtenberg, of the organized crime squad for Middle and West Brabant. Taking their name from the frog's Latin name, they called their investigation Aura.

Aura: a gentle breeze, a surrounding glow, a premonitory sensation experienced before an epileptic fit.

At first Ligtenberg had difficulty getting his men to take the case seriously; investigators felt a little silly working on frogs. But before long frogs evolved into turtles and lizards, and the countries involved moved in an arc across the world's Southern Hemisphere. Soon Ligtenberg's team members were phoning one another up at home, telling one another to turn on the television, watching *Animal Planet*–type programs together. They came into work in the mornings talking about what they had seen the night before. Something about animals sparked new enthusiasm in the group, and they laughed when they realized how true that was, even just for reptiles.

Best of all, it turned out that their tiny poison arrow frogs had pointed Team Aura toward a major international reptile-smuggling operation financed by an American company called Strictly Reptiles. The source for the reptiles was a Dutch expatriate living in Jakarta. A handful of men in the Breda area were involved in the operation, but they did not appear to be significant decision-makers. Andre Van Meer, however, was a world player, and so was his main buyer in the United States, Mike Van Nostrand. Van Nostrand appeared to be the smuggling ring's bank.

As a police officer, Ligtenberg understood what would happen if he took out the local Dutch middlemen: Andre Van Meer and Mike Van Nostrand would shift a corner of their smuggling triangle from Breda to Germany, or to the Czech Republic, or to some other country. Arresting Dutch locals would not stop the flow. Instead, they had to arrest the buyer, the seller, or both. After making calls to Interpol and to the U.S. Fish and Wildlife Service headquarters in Arlington, Virginia, Ligtenberg and another official boarded an airplane for the United States.

Under Dutch law, Team Aura could not work wildlife cases undercover. They did not have a powerful environmental law like the Lacey Act, either. On the other hand, Ligtenberg said, they did have the power to wiretap.

That they had been doing for almost a year, since early 1995.

It was a new situation for the U.S. Fish and Wildlife Service. Team Aura requested that the United States conduct searches and seizures at the premises of the subjects of their investigation. Authority for such a request lay in the countries' bilateral Mutual Legal Assistance Treaty, an agreement designed to cut through diplomatic red tape and allow prosecutors from one country to pursue fleeing defendants or hidden assets in another. It was believed to be the first time the U.S. government would carry out another country's MLAT request to investigate wildlife trafficking. Remarkably, Team Aura would be allowed to observe American investigators. U.S. authorities would be allowed to share in the fruits of the Dutch investigation.

Bepler listened to what the Dutch investigators had uncovered. Finally, the world had conspired in his favor. Mike Van Nostrand was guilty. All Bepler needed was proof.

Agent Eddie McKissick was first through the door. He wore a bulletproof vest, his Sig Sauer .45 at the ready. "Mike! Move away from the computer!"

McKissick was a muscular man with the voice of authority. Van Nostrand had burned him in the past, had embarrassed him, had yelled at him.

"Do it now!"

Jorge Picon entered; so did IRS agents, customs police, and a Dutch National Police officer who was a member of Team Aura. It seemed like the whole world was pouring into Strictly Reptiles. In fact, Strictly Reptiles was only a small part of what was going on. The nine A.M. raid on the Florida warehouse had been synchronized with raids on Van Nostrand's partners in New York, North Carolina, and New Mexico; ten locations in the Netherlands; and two in Indonesia.

Agents aware that Van Nostrand had a concealed-carry license secured the front office with vigor. To Van Nostrand it did not look like all of them were used to holding a live weapon.

Whoa! Whoa! he and his father yelled.

Agents ordered all hands in the air. They frisked everyone in the building, seizing guns, knives, and box cutters. Ray pointed to a flying gaff he used for fishing. "Do you want that?"

Agents ordered Van Nostrand's employees and customers outside and lined them up against the wall. One terrified customer turned to a friend of Mike's and asked, "Does this happen often?"

"All the time," the friend replied.

"No talking!" an agent yelled, and the customer clammed up; afterward, he would never be seen again.

Agent McKissick had an additional task. Snake hunter Art Bass, a sixty-one-year-old curmudgeon with half an arm missing from an alligator attack, lived somewhere inside the warehouse. It was well known that Bass kept firearms, but that is not what worried McKissick. The old man kept a deadly viper in his room. He would have to be not only disarmed but also unsnaked.

"What can I help you guys with?" Van Nostrand asked, quietly balling up evidence from the clipboard in his lap—handwritten notes about a shipment of turtles smuggled from Indonesia—and sliding it into his pocket. "Tell me what you're looking for and maybe I can help you find it."

The agents did not want his help. They wanted his knowledge. They were taking his files, his computer hard drives, his invoices. While one agent shot film of the warehouse, Jimmy Buffett, Ray's favorite musician, sang "Margaritaville" on an office stereo no one had switched off.

Ray Jr. leaned against the office countertop with his head down, one hand clutching the brim of his baseball cap. His eyes moved from his brother to his father to the agents storming their family.

For three and a half hours Mike Van Nostrand watched the government rifle through his things, his business, the place he had built. He joked a little during the search, but his face told a different story. He was as ashen as his white T-shirt. "Let me tell you something," he said. "If you didn't have them guns this shit would not be happening, because I got guns, too." On the back of the T-shirt was a drawing of a Japanese sumo wrestler, one leg raised in preparation for battle. On Van Nostrand the drawing seemed life-sized, a caricature of a massive, diapered baby stomping its foot.

"I understand you're a federal agent and all," he said to one man, "but you gotta show me something don't you?"

"Everything is sealed," the agent replied. Secrecy on the operation was extremely tight. Even Bepler's probable cause affidavit, the one he'd presented to the judge to get their search warrant, mentioned nothing about the Dutch investigation or the recordings the Dutch had made of Van Nostrand's conversations.

"It doesn't seem right," Van Nostrand complained.

It was a while before he realized that something else was not right.

"Where's Chip?" he asked his father.

Ray, who was taking the search in stride, leaning back

comfortably in a desk chair, thought for a moment. "If he's not here, bro, you can be sure he's at your house."

Michelle was in the shower when the telephone rang. As soon as Mike got home they were going to take the kids up to Disney World for the weekend. She was soaking wet when she picked up the telephone. "This is Special Agent Bepler," the caller said. "Would you please look out your window?"

Bepler squeezed his long legs into a coach seat on Delta Flight 38, headed for Amsterdam. His knees were crammed against the tray table. The raid on Strictly Reptiles had turned up no silver bullet. Bepler was not surprised. He had expected Mike to be too smart to leave evidence lying around. Still, the raid shook up Van Nostrand, and shut his mouth for a moment. But only for a moment. Already Van Nostrand was calling the raid "a fishing expedition," one that had caught no fish.

Regions 1 through 5, Special Operations, and head-quarters all were participating in the investigation now. Bepler had spent a month poring over records seized in the synchronized raids, and based on what he and others had found a new wave of subpoenas had gone out to busi-nesses tied to Strictly Reptiles in New York, New Jersey, Michigan, Missouri, and Texas.

His investigation was much bigger than Strictly Rep-tiles now, much bigger even than illegal reptile dealing in the United States. He was a part of a group of investigators extending from Miami to Breda to Jakarta, all working toward the same goal. Headquarters had dubbed the case the Netherlands Connection.

He arrived in Amsterdam just after eight A.M. on a Sunday morning. Already in town were Peter Murtha of the Justice Department's Wildlife and Marine Resources Section and Ernest Mayer, the new head of Special Operations, the tiny undercover squad inside Fish and Wildlife's headquarters.

Bepler was not sure about Mayer. Mayer might be the head of Special Operations, but he was from headquarters, and that made him a suit. Suits did not care about changing things long-term; they cared about headlines. On the day of the raid, Mayer had issued a press release titled "International Sweep Targets Reptile Smugglers," describing the efforts of the Netherlands, the United States, and Indonesia.

Maybe it was good to publicize the raid. Then again, maybe it wasn't.

Cooperation with Indonesia had already proved problematic. It would not have happened at all except that Dr. Willie Smits, who had helped the Dutch government in a case of smuggling of orangutans dubbed the Bangkok Six, was a naturalized Indonesian citizen and a personal adviser to the Minister of Forestry. For his work against wildlife smugglers, Smits, a kind of Thomas Jefferson for conservation and wildlife protection, had had several attempts made on his life.

Shortly before the Jakarta raid, a phone tap revealed that the targets knew the raid was coming. The information on the raid had been held so close that Smits believed only one person could have tipped Van Meer off. That person was an Indonesian CITES official. Still, Smits managed to assemble a small police unit, which raided Van Meer's home and Firma Hasco, and passed on the results to Team Aura.

Bepler and the American team sat down with Henry Ligtenberg's Team Aura. The Dutch described an international smuggling ring in exotic reptiles operating among Australia, Indonesia, the Netherlands, and the United States. They had tapes and transcripts documenting the entire operation. Frilled dragons, Fly River turtles, and other protected reptiles were smuggled out of Australia and remote parts of Indonesia to Firma Hasco, where they were routed through Van Meer's hometown in the Netherlands and sent on to Strictly Reptiles.

Team Aura turned over more than forty-five telephone conversations and faxes involving Strictly Reptiles. The conversations covered routes, payments, and other details. According to the Dutch investigators, Andre Van Meer was sending wild-caught frilled dragons to the Netherlands mislabeled as wild-caught crested geckos or hump-headed dragons. In Breda, middlemen held the lizards for several days to avoid the appearance of being a flow-through operation; then they shipped the lizards on to Strictly Reptiles labeled as frilled dragons that had been captive-bred in the Netherlands.

The Dutch had an added surprise. Team Aura had marked frilled dragons coming into Breda from Firma Hasco with what they called "special UV detection paste." Surreptitiously, they used a black light to monitor their suspects' outgoing shipments. The same lizards that came in labeled as wild-caught geckos were going out to Strictly

Reptiles as captive-bred frilled dragons. The proof was on video.

Bepler was overwhelmed. For over four years he had operated almost completely alone—buffeted by a paltry budget, aware that he was sucking resources from his friends in the office, haunted by the knowledge that he had stood at a fork in a road and had staked everything on a goal he might well not achieve and, worse, that if he failed to stop Van Nostrand nothing would change. Yet on the other side of the Atlantic, entirely unknown to him, others had been working to the same end, with the same passion.

Sitting in Holland, he listened to Team Aura's wiretap tapes. Here was Van Nostrand telling Dutch couriers to come in through New York to avoid the strict checks in Miami. Here was Van Nostrand screaming because animals were going to other dealers and not to him. Here was Van Nostrand pressing to corner the world market in the frilled dragon. And here, plain as day, was Van Nostrand telling his Dutch courier that if he got caught breaking the law Strictly Reptiles would pay his bail. Finally, in Breda, Bepler had found the knowledge he had been seeking for more than four years: guilty knowledge.

Fortress Malaysia

O kay," Anson Wong wrote to reptile importer Karl Hart, "I will offer you the same prices I offered to Strictly."

Karl Hart had wasted no time. Shunned by Van Nostrand at the National Reptile Breeders' Expo, he had returned home to Hawaii and written a letter to Anson Wong introducing himself and one of his companies.

Hart was a businessman. He had more money than most people would ever see in their lives, and he spent it on ventures that suited his fancy. Exactly how he made his money nobody he did business with ever knew exactly. What they did know was that whatever Karl Hart got into, he got into it to win. It didn't matter what the subject was. Hart was a big-game hunter. He was physical. His team had just won the grueling Molokai outrigger competition. He was six foot four and built like an upended

Lincoln Continental, a kind of Magnum, P.I., without the curly brown hair or the twinkling eyes. Hart's eyes were a bloodless ice blue. His seriousness was something people who knew him were quick to comment on—and, of course, the other thing that went along with that, the unspoken thing: Hart liked to get his hands bloody.

"The reptile and amphibian trade in the United States has increased substantially over the last ten years," Hart wrote in his introductory letter to Wong. He explained that his business, PacRim, was an established import-export company out of San Francisco and added, "We now wish to expand our market by making regular imports of high-quality reptiles."

It had not been difficult for Hart to decide where to go after Strictly Reptiles. Everybody knew the name Anson Wong. If you didn't, you could make your choice by geography. That is how Hart checked himself. He stuck the point of a mental protractor in Penang—Wong's headquarters—and opened it wide enough to catch Japan, the major Asian market for museum-quality reptiles; then he drew a circle. Every major opportunity—Australia, China, India, the UAE, Madagascar—was within Wong's reach. Put another way: if the endangered and most valuable reptiles of the Eastern Hemisphere were a target, Penang was its bull's-eye.

Hart had spent a year deciding where to locate his entrée into the reptile world. Hawaii was no good. It had too many restrictions on wildlife imports and was too isolated, both from source opportunities and from buyers. He'd seriously considered opening a business in Australia. Australia was home to more venomous snake species than any other country in the world. There was generally little money in venomous snakes but, by coincidence, Australia also had the world's most venomous conservation laws. Strict conservation rules meant that anything you got out of Australia had a good price on its head. Of course, getting it out was the challenge. Australia's wildlife cops were considered the best in the world.

Eventually he settled on San Francisco. It was a hike from his home in Hawaii, but San Francisco offered good port facilities, not much intrusion from competitors or from law enforcement, and it was not a bad place to live should he want to move there permanently. He rented an end unit in a small business park in Livermore, California, not far from Lawrence Livermore National Laboratory. He found the right man to staff the office, a reptile expert with a past as clouded as his own; ordered a fax machine; got an 800 number that disguised his true location; and hung a sign out front that read PACRIM.

Karl Hart was now in the international reptile wholesale business. He did not intend to stay in it for long. His goal was to see to see how high he could go and how much he could make.

What had impressed him from the beginning was that the reptile world was obviously run by various cartels. Asia, Africa, and South America were the resource states, and in those regions a couple of families and some lone individuals—living in Malaysia, Indonesia, Madagascar, Tanzania, and Suriname—controlled just about everything.

Southeast Asia was the choicest of these supplier regions. It had the most diverse species, the best mix of protective governments and inattentive ones, and a set of highly entrenched economic players—suggesting predictability and a substantial return for the man who could find himself a friend.

The feds were always making comparisons between

the animal trade and drugs. In that context, Southeast Asia is the Medellín cartel, only better. Besides the low penalties involved, there was a legal side to the reptile cartels—they put out price lists; they responded to solicitations. You could walk right in the front door and work your way up to the kind of business you wanted to do. Getting into any cartel was not that difficult as long as you knew the right people; Hart would let his money do the introductions.

First, he did his research. Not on reptiles—he knew less about them than he did about the ivory smuggling he had been involved in for a time. Karl Hart researched people. The top of the Southeast Asia cartel was occupied by Anson Wong, the Pablo Escobar of the live reptile trade.

Hart saw Malaysia as a fortress, with Wong in its castle. He liked that. Hart was a usurper of keeps, an opportunist, a man who fed on challenges. It was not just the money, it was the thrill of the game—like finding the best chess player in the world and playing him for cash, lots of cash. If the pieces on the board were iguanas and tortoises instead of bishops and castles, all the better. Sometimes a man as high up as Wong forgot what business he was in. Sometimes he thought, for example, that he was in the reptile business. Hart was not in the reptile business, the drug business, or any other business. He did not go in for bricks and mortar or bytes and data. He enjoyed walking into a man's castle, shaking his hand, and walking out with the crown jewel.

Knowing he needed some plausible background, Hart told Wong PacRim had been in business for several years

importing and wholesaling shells and coral for the aquarium and curio trade. He assumed Wong would not know
much about that.

Within two weeks of Hart's first letter, Wong wrote
back offering Hart giant coconut crabs for $125 apiece, as
well as "very realistic rubber (not plastic or silk) orchid
plants." Wong enclosed photographs of his coconut crabs,
which looked very much like hermit crabs that had been
irradiated to the size of Thanksgiving turkeys. Coconut
crabs, Hart learned, eat coconuts.

Hart passed on the crabs but asked for samples of the
rubber orchids. "Perhaps you could send samples with our
first shipment of reptiles," he suggested.

In less than a month Hart and Wong were correspond-
ing every few days, with Wong faxing short notes offering
reptiles—Burmese mountain tortoises, giant Aldabra tortoises direct from Mauritius, Fly River turtles—seemingly
as they came in to him. Within two months, Wong sent
Hart a fax offering him the same terms on a shipment of
tortoises that he gave to Strictly Reptiles.

To lay off the volume of purchases he knew he would
have to endure in order to work up to higher-end collect-
ibles, Hart took out an ad in *Reptiles* magazine:

ATTENTION JOBBERS: West Coast import/export company looking to establish long-term business rela-
tionships with jobbers in all 50 states. We import
mostly high-end herps from around the world.
Terms Available.

The ad included an 800 number, which reached Hart in
Hawaii.

He had no intention of becoming a business like Strictly Reptiles. He wanted to skim the cream off the reptile world, leaving the green iguanas and baby turtles to Mike Van Nostrand. There were tortoises out there worth $10,000; on the right lizard deal he could buy himself a new Hummer.

Because Hart knew so little about reptiles, he arranged it so that he and Wong communicated by fax; this way, Hart could compare prices with those offered by Strictly Reptiles and others and negotiate from there. He could also look at the laws in various countries and, by figuring out what was illegal, know what would be worth money or not, depending on its CITES paperwork. Anything he did not know he ran by his man in San Francisco.

Within three months Wong was offering Hart frilled dragons smuggled out of Indonesia and Papua New Guinea. Just before Hart's first shipment was scheduled to arrive, Wong contacted him and emphasized that the frilled dragons he was sending had all been captive-bred. Hart thought it was a strange thing to mention. He understood Wong's reasoning when, a few days later, the entire reptile world shook with news that the U.S. Fish and Wildlife Service and other authorities had raided Strictly Reptiles, Firma Hasco, and reptile businesses around the world.

Hardly a month passed before Wong had settled down again and began shipping Hart frilled dragons. Hart was now competing in one of the same black market species as Mike Van Nostrand. He knew he could not take all the credit for getting so far so quickly. The raid on Strictly Reptiles had no doubt stimulated Wong's interest in diversifying his American customer base. Still, luck came to those who made it, and Hart had done his homework. He could not go head-to-head with Van Nostrand; that would be foolish, anyway. Strictly Reptiles occupied the carnivore's point in the food chain: maximum energy if you ate the kill, nothing if you missed. Hart was happy to consume fewer calories for the sake of greater mobility. He did not intend to make a career out of reptiles.

Within six months of starting out, Hart was doing the sort of business with Wong that he had gotten into the reptile market for. It was easy to know what to focus on. On their price lists many of the major reptile dealers included plainly illegal species with the letters "CB" next to the price, standing for captive-bred—often shorthand, Hart figured out, for smuggled. He could also look at the cover of *Reptiles* to see what was hot. Just before he contacted Wong, the September 1995 issue had featured the frilled dragon. Anything on the cover of *Reptiles* sold well. He checked dealers' Web sites, too.

Hart tried to get Wong to introduce him to some people in Australia he could travel to meet, but Wong was not interested. "These people, most of them are ex-convicts, and they shoot buffalos for a living," Wong said of his suppliers. "They're wild people and occasionally we receive things from them." His suppliers were not interested in meeting a new guy. Same with Firma Hasco, which Hart also asked Wong about.

"I will ask Firma Hasco on your behalf . . . but they are already firmly established in the West Coast so that could be the reason for not being interested in your inquiries," Wong explained. He and Mohamad Hardi were very good friends, he assured Hart. "Let me know the quantities you want, and I will try to get you prices."

Hart asked Wong to procure for him a rare and protected

Philippine lizard called the Gray's monitor. The Gray's monitor is the only primarily fruit-eating monitor lizard in the world. It had been thought extinct until it was rediscovered in the 1970s, and so it was a bit of a hit among monitor lizard collectors. Wong had just sold a dozen of them. He said he'd gotten them through an arrangement he had with Malaysia's Department of Wildlife and National Parks. A smuggler had been busted coming in from Bangkok with a suitcaseful. The Department of Wildlife had called Wong and asked him to identify the lizards; he had, and the government had confiscated the lizards. "They confiscate animals," Wong told Hart, "and sell them to me. Legally!"

Hart suggested that maybe they could smuggle some Gray's monitor lizards over to San Francisco in a hidden compartment. "Wow," Wong said. He never did that sort of thing, he told Hart. He had too much to lose.

"But," he added slyly, "my workers have accidentally packed something that wasn't meant to be shipped. That has happened sometimes."

Wong hatched a small plan: Hart would buy a couple hundred Tokay geckos from him. "You know how Tokays like to jump up when you open the bag, or the box?" he said. Wong would fill fifty little cotton boxes with biting and jumping Tokay geckos and put them on top of a shipment of Gray's monitors. Nobody would go through that many Tokays, he said. It was a trick he and Mike Van Nostrand used from time to time. "You take two hundred," Wong told Hart. "I'll send you a hundred no charge."

Van Nostrand was still buying from Wong, but he was keeping their relationship clean until he found out what

Bepler planned to do. Not that Van Nostrand was giving up. He was suing Bepler, along with the director of the U.S. Fish and Wildlife Service and Attorney General Janet Reno, demanding return of his Indian star tortoises. The tortoises had cost him about $15,000 (which he had secretly paid directly to Wong). The best, and worst, part about suing Bepler was that all ninety-eight Indian star tortoises were dead. Van Nostrand had found out by chance from a customer that the tortoises had died on the premises of the custodian Bepler had taken them to. Mike's lawyers were sending letters to the government offering to care for the tortoises, reminding officials that reptiles they had seized in the past had died, laying a foundation for the jury trial Van Nostrand intended to demand.

The thing that Hart could do that Van Nostrand could not do, or would not do, was pay on time. For Wong, that meant a great deal. When Hart said he would pay, he paid, by wire transfer directly to Wong's account at the Hongkong and Shanghai Banking Corporation (HSBC), Penang.

Wong offered to make Hart sole U.S. distributor for the radiated tortoise, an endangered, Appendix I tortoise from Madagascar. He was already shipping radiated tortoises to Japan hidden under large water monitors, nasty lizards that Japanese inspectors notoriously feared. He offered the same opportunity to Hart.

Hart had reached the castle gate. It had taken him only a year. He accepted and began smuggling in radiated tortoises; he sold them for $1,500 apiece. Wong even helped him find buyers, including some in Florida, in Strictly Reptiles' backyard.

For some Indonesian species, Wong said he could bribed CITES officials in Malaysia to change Latin names on export permits. The Malaysian CITES authorities, Wong explained, were generally well respected around the world. He assured Hart that once he got his animals past CITES, greasing a few additional palms along the way, they were home free.

When Hart requested Timor pythons, the rare species Van Nostrand had smuggled home in his shorts, Wong asked for two weeks to put the project together. Then he demonstrated why people considered him not just a smuggler but an architect.

"Okay," Wong said by telephone, "here is the way it's going to be done. I will have a fall guy and he will get arrested. Plus the goods will be confiscated and the goods will be sold to me by the department. Once they are sold . . . they are deemed legal!"

The Timor pythons would come with CITES papers! Even Van Nostrand was unable to do that.

"I love looking at all these little loopholes and taking advantage of it," Wong told Hart.

"Yes, me too," Hart said.

Wong laughed. "Laws are made to be broken," he said. It was a line that got both men laughing together.

A few weeks before Christmas 1996, Wong offered to sell Hart the rarest tortoise on earth. Somewhere between three hundred and one thousand Madagascan plowshare tortoises were believed to exist in the wild. Outside of the Honolulu Zoo, no plowshare tortoises were known to exist in the United States. Earlier in the year, thieves had stolen seventy-three juveniles and two adult females from a Malagasy breeding facility in the Ampijoroa Forest Reserve run by the Jersey Wildlife Preservation Trust.

Hart was worried that the stolen tortoises might be marked in some way, but Wong assured him that they were not; just in case, he had run an electromagnet over them to scramble the data on any microchips. He told Hart he had been offered forty-six plowshare tortoises, twenty-three pairs. According to Wong, a German turtle expert from the Dresden Museum had been shot near the compound, and Wong suggested that he had been involved in the theft. There had been three Germans, he said. One had been shot in the ass, another killed. Who knew what the real story was, he mused.

In any case, Wong was keeping the largest two tortoises for himself, and he offered a pair to Hart for $13,000. Hart countered with $11,000, and they settled on $11,500. These were not the stolen plowshares, Wong added.

Later Hart learned that Malagasy authorities had shot and killed two German reptile collectors, blinding a third. The incident had occurred three years earlier and did not involve plowshares. Wong was lying about his source for the tortoises, but Hart didn't care. Wong's story underscored the stakes involved in high-end reptile smuggling. It made Hart giddy.

To smuggle the tortoises to the States, Wong contacted a friend who he said "runs" Asian girls to people in "the flesh trade" or "white slavery" in the United States and Europe. The friend declined, saying it was better to stick with the girls. On February 19, 1997, Hart received two plowshares from Wong hidden inside a shipment of legal reptiles.

And that was all it took for Karl Hart for climb to the top of the illegal reptile world and enter the fortress.

Hart did not want to double his money on frilled dragons by the hundreds. He wanted genetic masterpieces, single species hanging in their own room at the end of evolutionary hallways. He was a modern version of Hank Molt, interested only in the ungettable. There was one reptile species that even Hank Molt considered outside the bounds of good smuggling: New Zealand's tuatara.

Hart wanted some.

Among reptile hobbyists, the tuatara has an almost religious standing. Set off on a page of its own in even the most basic children's reptile book, the tuatara is a kind of symbolic bridge between the plastic dinosaurs many reptile lovers started out playing with as children and the living world these herpetophiles came to admire. Often described as a "living fossil," the tuatara is unique. They have no external ears; their ribs are structured like birds'; and males lack a penis, forcing them to partner in a mixing of fluids and hope. They resemble a cross between a lizard and a primitive fish. Like many lizard species, tuataras possess a "third eye" on top of the head; it has a lens, a retina, and nerve connection to the brain. But while the third eye in other lizards helps in the regulating of body temperature, the function of the third eye in the tuatara is not known and may even have some ability to see. Some Maori consider the tuatara a sacred boundary symbol, not to be crossed. For a time, its image was on the New Zealand five-cent coin.

To get tuataras, Wong contracted the world's most

famous tuatara poacher, Freddie Angell of New Zealand. Angell had already been convicted once for burglary of the Southland Museum and Art Gallery tuatarium, in which he'd attempted to steal three of the rarer form of the species, the Brother's Island tuatara, whose wild population was less than three hundred. Angell was relentless for tuataras, addicted to them in a way that made even men like Hart and Wong raise their eyebrows. Angell simply wanted all of them.

Wong put up the money for Angell's boats and nets and sent him a false-bottomed shipping crate; as a down payment Hart wired $2,000. To ensure the heist's success, Wong designed a backup plan: he would send into New Zealand two locals from Penang posing as tourists. He mailed Hart a travel brochure with the package their poachers would sign up for circled. Hart chipped in for that, too.

Instead of reptiles, bad news came back from New Zealand: Angell had been caught red-handed and had confessed—everything. Wong told Hart not to worry. He had put ten grand in to match Hart's five, and he was not worried. The *Timaru Herald* was reporting that Angell had identified Anson Wong as his co-conspirator, and still, Wong was not worried. The two locals had not done anything and Wong had papered over his connection to Angell with receipts for sheepskins. There was no way anyone could prove his connection to Angell. Besides, who would believe Angell? Just in case, Wong promised to remove Hart's file from his business. He assured Hart that his telephones were not tapped; nevertheless, he told Hart, they should continue to speak in code. The word for tuataras was *televisions*.

At his home in Hawaii, Hart could only shake his head in awe. There was no getting over Wong. He was irrepressible. The music that played on Wong's telephone when he put Hart on hold was the theme song from the movie *The Sting*. Wong said there was nothing any cop in the world could do to stop him as long as he stayed in Malaysia. "I could sell a panda and nothing," he told Hart. "As long as I'm still here I'm safe."

Hart and Wong talked openly about Strictly Reptiles now, and they agreed that Mike Van Nostrand was an obnoxious person to deal with. Discord between Wong and Van Nostrand was good news for Hart. What was true of a biological ecosystem was also true of an economic one: take out a player and you altered the future. You opened a niche for an enterprising competitor, like Karl Hart. The raid on Strictly and its partners in Europe and Indonesia had changed the dynamics of the international reptile market. Karl Hart was a key beneficiary of the unsettled moment Agent Bepler and Team Aura had created. With Strictly in the crosshairs of U.S. Fish and Wildlife, buying patterns, credit terms, prices, and collected species had shifted, and the government had not even arrested Van Nostrand yet.

Wong proved ingenious at packaging star tortoises into long sausages and hiding them among large monitor lizards, rendering them virtually invisible. He played with the Latin names of protected species, relying on the looseness of the Malaysian language, which did not always distinguish between a species and its protected subspecies. There were limits to Wong's confidence, however:

he refused to ship high-profile species from Penang. Anything he deemed risky, he had sent from either mainland Malaysia or other countries, such as Indonesia.

Hart and Wong continued to build their partnership. They enlisted a corrupt Federal Express employee in Arizona, who arranged fake drops for shipments from Wong. They used a somewhat deluded ex-lawyer and avowed Deadhead from Ohio named James Burroughs as their human courier. Burroughs, who worked as a canvasser for small NGOs, such as Clean Water Action, rationalized his smuggling after seeing a *National Geographic* article on the death of the "lungs of the world," the rain forests of Southeast Asia, more of which were burned each year at the hands of development.

On Burroughs's first trip to Penang, Wong had the second-ranked customs official on the island pick the courier up at the airport and drive him to Wong's office. It cemented Burroughs's awe of the man he soon referred to as "the godfather" and "Dean Wong."

Wong was wary of Burroughs, a man he did not know. He did not hand him anything illegal directly, but instead had an intermediary deliver reptiles to Burroughs's hotel room, with a message that the animals were not from Anson.

Wong also warned Hart not to meet with Burroughs directly. It was too dangerous, he advised.

Hart ignored Wong's advice. Eager to put his hands on new species, Hart flew to Chicago and met Burroughs as he exited customs at O'Hare. Burroughs was wearing a blue sport coat over a yellow T-shirt that read "S.P.E.R.M." The T-shirt was classic Wong, funny and in your face.

"We are not the 'droids you're looking for, move

along," Burroughs was saying to himself as he passed out of customs.

"Hey, James," Hart said.

"How you doing?"

They walked for a bit.

Burroughs began to ramble, using words like *thusly* and *jeopardy* and *in good faith*. Hart did not quite understand what the man was talking about. He led Burroughs outside to his rental car and then drove him to the Radisson Inn, where Hart had a room. Burroughs laid his suitcase on the bed and opened "Big Blue," the suitcase Wong had bought for him. Inside were illegal tortoises balled into socks—ten Indian star tortoises in one brown sock, four Burmese star tortoises in another. A third tortoise-filled sock was destined for some other buyer. Burroughs also removed from the suitcase a plastic container with five long-snouted crocodilians called false gharials inside.

On his next trip Burroughs brought home a tortoise; two Chinese alligators, each in a sock; and a baby Komodo dragon. Komodo dragons are the world's largest lizards, giant deer-eating land alligators with striking intelligence. They are born larger than most lizard species will ever grow. Hart paid twelve grand for the baby Komodo dragon and believed he could sell it for thirty. He ordered another one. Burroughs would bring in that one, too.

Hart tired of reptiles. If he counted up only the black market species, he figured he had earned about $371,000 on animals that had cost him just over $51,000. The plow-share tortoise; the tuatara; Appendix I and II reptiles from Madagascar, Indonesia, China, India, Fiji, the Philippines:

Hart had picked the lock on nature's art gallery and plundered its rooms of the world's Vermeers, Rembrandts, and Picassos.

No one could say Karl Hart was not a player now. There was not a reptile species in the world he could not get through Anson Wong. All that was left was routine, like what Strictly Reptiles had. That was the problem with raiding art galleries and storming castles: in the end you were left standing in an empty room.

Hart was through with reptiles, but it was not his style to squander an asset he had worked so hard to acquire.

He decided to branch out.

"I got a couple of new business ventures here that I need to discuss with you sometime," he told Wong. What he was thinking about, he said, was dealing in bear gallbladders, whose bile was a coveted ingredient in traditional Chinese medicine. They could get $25 to $30 an ounce for bear galls, brokered by the right man in Asia, he told Wong.

Wong said he would look into it. Two days later he wrote Hart, "My client has given an indication of how much he will pay...US $3.80 per gram for the top grade (Golden colour like maple syrup or honey shades) and US $.50 for the Greens or Black." An ounce, Wong pointed out, contained twenty-eight grams.

Bear gallbladders were too dangerous an item to do business in directly, Wong said. Depending on what Hart had in mind, Wong would work something out with a man in a "very high position in Government office."

Hart did not want to tell Wong too much. He had a business contact in Vancouver, a woman who was savvy in the ways of getting things done. "I aim to make this one of the largest if not the largest animal companies in the West, filling the void left by Tommy and others," he said. He did not have to say who Tommy was. Crutchfield was the reason Wong could not visit the United States. He did not have to say who "others" were, either. Everyone knew Mike Van Nostrand and his father were in serious trouble.

As he had done with reptiles, Hart wanted to keep his new exotic-mammals operation exclusive. Wong was his first choice to supply the venture.

Wong loved the idea. He agreed that they should take things to a new level and concentrate their business on "top-dollar, hard-to-find things."

Wong had contacts all over the world, and his reach extended well beyond reptiles. He had offered Hart the horns of the Sumatran rhinoceros in both whole and ground form. The Sumatran rhino was the world's smallest rhinoceros, carried two horns, and, according to Wong, was more desirable for medicinal uses than African varieties. Wong offered black palm cockatoos from Australia. He boasted his access to snow leopard pelts and pandas. He offered shahtoosh, which translated correctly means "the king of wool," made from the hair of the Tibetan chiru antelope, an Appendix I animal. He had available a marbled cat, a housecat-sized animal with the coat of a clouded leopard. When Hart mentioned he had heard that Wong could get him a Spix's macaw, Wong said he'd sold his already. One went to Singapore, and two went to Spain.

To get the gallbladders operation going, Wong suggested that they bring in a retired government veterinarian who used to sign export permits for him. He was the man Wong had consulted to learn the prices of the different gallbladder grades.

Privately, Hart was not interested in bringing in anyone new until he was certain Wong would get along with his Canadian partner. It was time to meet up together and map out their new direction. Wong was hesitant. There was an arrest warrant out on him in the United States. He was sure that if the U.S. government caught him, they would want him to stay a long, long time. He asked Hart, "Would they have a system in that computer with my details on it if I was to land in Vancouver?"

Hart was no lawyer. "I assume they would in the U.S.," he said. "But I don't know why Canada would." They agreed: the meeting would take place in Canada.

Karl Hart, whose true identity was George Morrison, special agent for the U.S. Fish and Wildlife Service, was thrilled. Karl Hart had put together a wonder closet of rare animals over the past three years. George Morrison was a collector of species even more rare than the animals Hart had acquired; Morrison aspired to a collection of one. After nearly three years of undercover work, George Morrison was about to get his jewel.

Wong called in a panic. He had in his hand a press release about a global U.S. Fish and Wildlife sting operation involving the new arrest of Tommy Crutchfield, two Germans operating out of Madagascar, and others. Wong read the press release to Hart. Near the end was the part that made Wong nervous: "In addition to the charges against Crutchfield and his associates, four individuals from Germany, South Africa, Canada, and Japan have been arrested and successfully prosecuted in the United States."

"So, you see, this little three-line sentence—'in addition to these charges in the U.S., authorities in Germany *and Canada,*'" he said, emphasizing the last, "this was the sentence that made me feel queasy."

Wong well knew his status in the United States. He told Hart that the American penalty for trading in endangered CITES animals was five years in prison and a $250,000 fine. "I am not sure where I stand with the old problems," he wrote in an e-mail to Hart, "but I am not about to take any chances. . . . I would really be a feather in the cap for USFW that brings me in." Hart agreed; Canada was out.

Wong offered alternatives. "We can meet anywhere here in Asia, or the Pacific Rim or Argentina, Johannesburg, Peru, or Paris, England or anywhere in Europe," Wong wrote. "You name the place. . . . No New Zealand or Australia."

Hart suggested Mexico. Some fun in the Acapulco sun sounded good to both of them. But again, with just days remaining until their meeting, Wong wanted to back out.

"I have a bad feeling with Mexico . . . maybe just nerves?" Wong wrote shortly before his trip. "I wonder if people in USFW monitors [*sic*] computers and msgs.?? Please convince me I am worried over nothing? Adios, Anson."

Wong was a prisoner in his own castle, afraid to step into the light. It was amusing, really, for a reptile man to have a phobia.

"These people FWS, are not the CIA or FBI," Hart wrote Wong. "They can't do an adequate job of inspecting shipments. I don't know how they could monitor the thousand or millions of Computer messages."

Besides, he asked, "If they want you so bad why wouldn't they just have your country nab you and send you over here?"

Wong and Hart agreed to meet with Hart's partner in Mexico City first and leave Acapulco for later. Once they'd ironed out their new business, Wong said, he would fly to Madagascar to pick up some valuable tortoises.

They would all rendezvous at the airport in Mexico City. Wong said he would be wearing a black T-shirt emblazoned with a white iguana head. Normally, for trips like this, he liked to wear a baseball cap to use as a signal. If he came off the plane not wearing the cap, anyone planning to meet him would know there had been trouble, and should ignore him. He did not intend to wear one on this trip, though. There would be no need. Hart said he would have on the 1996 National Reptile Breeders' Expo T-shirt. It was black with a bunch of snakes on the front and the word "Expo" written in big red letters.

At approximately seven-thirty P.M., Japan Airlines Flight 12 arrived at gate 23 in Mexico City International Airport. On his way up to the immigration booth, Wong paused to tie his shoe. He had on a pair of faded blue jeans, a light blue jacket, and, as promised, a black T-shirt with a white iguana head.

A pair of cowboy boots appeared next to his foot. It was Hart. Wong stood up and fixed his glasses. "At last a face to match the voice," he said, and shook Hart's hand.

It seemed strange how close Karl Hart was to him as they walked forward toward immigration. Stranger still that Hart was on this side of the immigration counter.

Wong tried to remember when Hart was supposed to have arrived in Mexico City.

They were about halfway to the immigration booth when Mexican authorities broke their line and directed the two men to the nearest open booth. Hart presented his passport to immigration first; then Wong showed his.

As Wong stepped into Mexico, Operation Chameleon, a three-year U.S. Fish and Wildlife Service undercover investigation involving hundreds of thousands of dollars, a false business, several agents, zoo cooperation, and authorities in Canada, Mexico, Australia, and New Zealand, pulled a king from his castle. Special Agent George Morrison had walked into Fortress Malaysia and walked out with reptile smuggling's crown jewel.

He had taken care of supply. Bepler's job was demand.

Caged

Mike Van Nostrand got to work early, already in a miserable mood. Michelle had missed her last period. Plus, twelve months had passed since Bepler's fishing expedition; an arrest was coming. He just did not know when. He thought about that every single day, and it showed. He had dark circles under his eyes. The flesh on his face sagged.

It was barely after eight A.M. when his telephone rang. It was Michelle again. "You're not going to like this," she said.

"Uh-oh," Van Nostrand heard a worker who was in already say.

He looked up. Across the office his employee began backing away from the front door.

"Michelle," Van Nostrand said.

From outside he could hear car doors slamming. Eddie McKissick's deep voice filled the office, ordering the employee to stay where he was.

"Michelle," Van Nostrand repeated. "I'm going to have to call you back."

Agent McKissick entered with colleagues Van Nostrand did not recognize.

"It's time, Mike," McKissick said. He had Van Nostrand stand and put his hands behind his back.

The handcuffs caught on Mike's Rolex. He had to turn and undo the double clasp, and so for a moment he and McKissick were working together to get the handcuffs onto his wrists. It was a relief. After a year of not knowing when they would be coming, the moment had finally arrived. An agent searched his pockets. He pulled out a roll of bills worth about $2,000 and dropped it on a desk.

McKissick started to move Mike toward the door.

"You're not gonna leave that there, are you?" Van Nostrand asked. He said it would be all right for his employee to hold it for him, so agents called the employee back into the room and handed him the cash.

"What's this, a bribe?" the young man demanded. It got Van Nostrand to laugh.

"Where's Chip?" he asked.

"Well," McKissick said, "he figured maybe it would be better if I just arrested you myself."

"I want to thank you for not doing this at my house, in front of my wife and kids," Van Nostrand said.

"That wasn't my decision," McKissick said. "That was Chip's decision."

Van Nostrand swallowed. He had hated Bepler. If the situation had been reversed, he would have considered this the moment to savor, the takedown. He might even have made the arrest at a public place, to humiliate Bepler.

But that was not what Bepler had done. The day was still quiet. His children were still at home, safe.

In a world of takers, his enemy had given him what a flesh peddler rarely got. Besides, he had to admit, Chip had been right 90 percent of the time. He'd even been right about the star tortoises. They weren't captive-bred, but they looked it, and they had paperwork. Even if he was wrong, he argued to himself, he was just as right as Bepler was.

Bepler was in the room for McKissick at that moment, too. "It's important to treat people as people," Bepler had counseled him more than once. McKissick had come to his job with a more physical approach, more like his view on corporal punishment for children, over which they also disagreed. "People can break the law and still be people," Bepler said.

McKissick sat Van Nostrand in the back of a government car. They had not come only for Mike.

"Where's Dale Marantz?" an agent asked.

Marantz and Mike's father were on their way in to work. "I don't know where Dale is," Mike replied.

He was still sitting in the back of the car when he glimpsed Dale's black vehicle pulling into the lot. Ray was in the passenger seat. Van Nostrand watched the car pull in, then stop. The agents in front of him were talking, comparing how much time they had left until retirement. That was something Van Nostrand would never forget, the focus these men had on retirement. It reinforced his belief that you went to work for the government not for the good you could do but for the benefits. Why else would you do it? Van Nostrand watched as the black car slowly backed up, then took off. Just as it passed the building, one of the agents turned.

"Who was that?" he asked Mike.

"Who was what?"

"That car that just went—"

"Dude, I don't know," Van Nostrand said. "I don't have my glasses."

Fish and Wildlife eventually found Marantz, and Van Nostrand got him a lawyer. "They're not going to give you more time than they give me," he told Marantz. Dale should keep his mouth shut and sit tight until they figured out what was going to happen to Mike. If he didn't, it would be a lot worse for all of them. Worst case, Mike would pay him to sit in prison; the going rate to keep a witness in jail with his mouth closed was $5,000 per month, he told Marantz.

It was obvious, Van Nostrand's lawyer argued later that same day, that his client was not a flight risk. "Your honor," Patrick O'Brien said, "he's been under investigation for the past five years—if he was gonna go anywhere, he would have left a long time ago."

The judge agreed. Pending trial, he ordered a signature bond and let Van Nostrand out on conditional release.

Ten months later Judge K. Michael Moore sentenced Van Nostrand to eight months in federal prison and took away his export license. Marantz got one month. The judge ordered Strictly Reptiles to pay nearly $250,000 to Indonesia's World Wildlife Fund. (Van Nostrand had wanted his fine to go to save African gorillas.)

"Your honor," O'Brien cried out, "we can't pay that. We're not smuggling anymore!"

Prosecutors had wanted more time for Van Nostrand.

They had come at him from both the Environmental Crimes Section Chris McAliley had started in Miami and from Justice Department headquarters' Wildlife and Marine Resources Section, the unit inspired by Hank Molt. By the time the Strictly Reptiles investigation had momentum, McAliley had moved on to private practice. Assistant U.S. Attorney Tom Watts-Fitzgerald prosecuted the case. Without Miami's Environmental Crimes Section, Bepler would never have made the cases that got him to Strictly, and he would never have made the cases that came next.

As part of his plea, Van Nostrand admitted to wrongs known and unknown to the government, and committed to assisting Bepler in cases against other reptile smugglers. His crimes had been, after all, just a bookkeeper's adventure.

With Van Nostrand's help, Bepler and Watts-Fitzgerald took down many of Strictly Reptiles' South Florida smuggling partners, including the cruise-ship smugglers and Phil Langston. Ripples went out across the world. Arrests were made in the Netherlands, Indonesia, and Germany. Just as Strictly Reptiles' success at smuggling had acted as a green light to smugglers of all kinds, its fall seemed to energize criminal investigations everywhere. Reptile smugglers went down in South Africa, Cameroon, and Canada.

Bepler did something for Van Nostrand, too. The case he pursued never really touched Ray, whose iguana smuggling and ties to the Tabraue narcotics organization and criminal history would have made him a newsworthy target. The deal Mike struck with the government cast an umbrella of protection over his father. It was something Mike would laugh about eventually: his dad broke the rules, and Mike got in trouble for it.

Mike's family had a going-away party for him. He kept hoping something would happen and he would not have to go. It was the same thought he'd had that night in the garage before his father went away to prison. He had three children of his own now, two boys and a girl. If only something or someone would intercede.

The next morning, a Monday, his father picked him up in his truck and they began their drive to prison. The day never really opened, staying overcast and cool. It was a six-hour trip up to Jesup, Georgia. They drove past exits for Fort Pierce, where they had first moved so Ray could catch indigo snakes. They drove past exits for Disney World, a trip Mike never took that day Fish and Wildlife raided his company and his home.

They talked a little about the business. Mike's mom was going to come in to help. Things would run the way they always had. In no time, he would be back.

It would not be that bad, his father told him. Federal prison? You got television in your room, movies on Friday nights. If they had pussy in there, Ray liked to joke, he would sign himself back in. But, really, what was there to say? It had never bothered Ray that his son was smuggling. Everybody did it.

Ray had grown up in the animal business, and as far as he knew there was not a major reptile importer in the country who did not at some point get his hands dirty smuggling. Their biggest competitors were *still* doing it. When you got right down to it, he believed, we're all going to be extinct someday.

A part of Ray was even glad Mike was going away. The government had saved Ray's life by sending him to prison back in his drug-trafficking days. If they had not stopped him, he would have kept at it, even though cocaine was making people do some crazy things and the guys he was working with were getting more and more violent. The government had taken him out of the cocaine business. In a way, Bepler's catching Mike was saving his life a second time, and probably Mike's, too.

Ray loved his son.

They arrived at Jesup Federal Correctional Institution a little before noon. Mike was going to the camp, the minimum-security facility next door, but it all looked the same driving up.

"Holy shit!" the intake guard said. "He's loaded. Look at all the money he's got."

Van Nostrand had done the math on what he would need for an eight-month stay. He figured three grand ought to cover things. It turned out that was a lot more money than most men walked in with. They gave him a toothbrush and a new set of clothes.

The group of men surrendering that day talked to one another about what they'd heard it was like, what they were sure they were going to do, what they were not going to do. Lingering in the air were the questions everyone has about prison life.

"Gentlemen," an older man announced, "I want you to know that you're looking at the only innocent man in this cell." He was connected somehow to a coffee company, in on mail fraud or a land deal of some kind. A tall, husky black man sat to the side, not saying much. He had the resigned look of a senior in a room full of freshmen.

Van Nostrand was assigned to Dormitory B, Room 4.

When he got to his cell, a cement cubical built for two, he looked across the hall and saw the laconic senior.

His name was Baker, he said.

The "cells" at the Jesup camp resembled college dormitory rooms without doors. You stepped down into your room, which had a set of bunk beds and two dressers. His cubemate, convicted for something to do with illegal cell phones, was in the hole when Mike arrived, so Mike took the lower bunk and the better dresser.

He made friends with Baker, who was in for a probation violation on an underlying crime that had something to do with automatic weapons. Mike heard that a lot: "something to do with." You didn't pry. Most guys were in for drugs. There were a lot of father-son redneck teams from Georgia in for pot. A lot of those.

You had to have a job. Van Nostrand put in to be a mechanic. Baker said, "Why? You have to get up at six A.M., work in grease, spend all day in the hot sun."

Baker knew the supervisor and got Van Nostrand a job in the kitchen scrubbing pots and pans.

He had only one goal for his time away. He weighed 352 pounds. He started jogging soon after he arrived, intent, just as his father had been during his incarceration, to drop some weight.

"Hey, Slow Motion!" he heard from a prisoner. "Hey, Slow Motion, what are you in for?"

"Turtles," he replied.

At first they couldn't believe it, but then they remembered that another reptile smuggler, a guy named Tom Crutchfield, had served time at Jesup; so had some orangutan smuggler.

"Slow Motion's killing babies!" he heard while taking a shower, and learned the prison slang for masturbation. "Stop cube peeping, Slow Motion!"

He did not have much trouble. In the morning he would wake up to oranges bouncing into his room, Baker tossing them from across the hall. Get up, go eat, hit the track, shower, sleep, run, scrub pots and pans, eat, scrub pans, work out, run around the track, go to bed. Six to nine miles a day. He had a guy doing his laundry; another guy cleaned his room. For personal training, he paid Ironhead a six-pack of soda every week or so and whatever candy bars the big man stole from his locker. They called him Ironhead because he was in a fight one time and the other guy hit him in the head with a pipe; that was the last thing the other guy remembered. Ironhead bench-pressed a drug-free 575.

The thing is, Mike realized, in prison you can't let anyone know that anything bothers you. Nothing. "Jodie's servicing your wife," prisoners would yell to each other. Jodie was the name for the guy you wondered about while you were away.

"Hey, Slow Motion," a man asked one day, "will you get me a soda?"

"Yeah," he said, and handed the man his vending machine card.

"They're just trying to see what they can get off you," one of the guys chided him.

"Look, bro," he shot back, "if a guy wants a fucking soda, I don't fucking give a shit. He's not coming up to me every hour. What the fuck do I care? It's fifty cents."

Another man came up and grabbed him. "Buy me a soda."

Van Nostrand weighed more than most prisoners, but

he was not a physical man. All he had was his mouth. He was afraid of this man they called B, and afraid, too, of what would happen if he backed down.

"Look, B," he said. "If you want a soda, I'll get you a soda. But are you asking because you want a soda or because you want to see if I'll buy you one?" It led to a scuffle. Van Nostrand asked Baker to tell B to leave him alone; that was all it took.

Time stood still, and he tried to kill it. He went with Baker to a Nation of Islam meeting to listen to Louis Farrakhan on tape. "What did you think?" the men asked him. "How do you listen to that?" he replied. "He's telling you not to do what he does."

Van Nostrand and Baker talked about the differences in their backgrounds. Baker referred to him as Michael. He pointed at the lunch line one day and said, "Michael, how many black people do you see there?"

"Hardly any."

"That's right. Why is it that eighty percent of the prisons are Hispanic and black and all you see in that line is white people?"

The answer was that all the blacks were in "fucking FCI," the more restricted part of the prison, across the street. You could see it, right there in front of you, Mike thought. You take two guys, one black and one white, identical crimes, and the black guy got the harder sentence every time. Baker got Mike thinking about things. Baker wrote to Michelle and told her not to worry.

Michelle brought the kids up, even though he'd told her not to. He had not let her bring them to his sentencing, the way some defendants did. His mother had read a statement that day. She was tearful, and so was he. Even Bepler said later how heart-wrenching her speech had been. Your mother was one thing, but Mike did not want sympathy at the expense of his children.

His daughter, who was the oldest, seemed okay, but his three-year-old son scowled in a furious way that was familiar. "What are you doing here?" his son demanded in a voice balled like a fist.

Michelle had brought their baby, too. Van Nostrand turned from his older son to look at his baby's little boots. He stared at the tiny shoes of a small boy.

"When are you coming home?" his son demanded.

Van Nostrand just stared at his baby's tiny shoes.

If you wanted food from the outside, the price was one for one. Prisoners with family living in the Jesup area would arrange to have food smuggled onto the prison grounds at night. Whatever food you ordered cost you double the menu price. Paying for smuggled food could be done a variety of ways. You could pay the inmate who arranged the transaction by buying him things at the commissary. Mike supplemented his personal training fees to Ironhead that way, buying Ironhead a new pair of running shoes, for example. The inmate who cleaned Mike's cube had a wife serving time in another prison. She needed money so instead of paying for his cleaning service directly, Mike arranged for his own wife, Michelle, to make deposits to the inmate's wife's account. Cash was not allowed in prison. The money Mike had walked in with on his first day had been taken from him and deposited in his commissary account. Still, you could get cash in, and it was the preferred currency among outside couriers.

Money was handed over quickly, shuffled through hands when the guards weren't looking, brought in and paid out in much the same way as the food came in.

Prison was good for his health, although his diet was spotty. More than once guards on the morning shift found shrimp tails or a KFC bucket in the trash. He served five months.

He heard what they were saying while he was away. *Mike's in, jail, Strictly is going downhill. Strictly's going out of business.*

He walked out of prison weighing 262 pounds. He had lost ninety pounds. His blood pressure had dropped forty points. His nosebleeds were gone.

Under his sentence, he lost his export license for five years, but he could petition Fish and Wildlife to get it back after three. Three years later he applied to get it back. No matter who he talked to at Fish and Wildlife, he knew the decision was going to be Bepler's to make.

"How do we know you won't repeat your crimes?" they asked him.

"It cost me a lot of aggravation," he told them. "A lot of money and a lot of time. But you don't have a guarantee.

"If I do it again," he said, "it's gonna be for a lot of money. I'd have to make five or six hundred thousand dollars on the deal. And that won't happen," he added quickly. "In the animal business you can't make that kind of money. It's not possible. There's no five- or six-hundred-thousand animal deal."

At the time, he was telling the truth.

Special Agent

Bepler was back at his real desk, a cubicle upstairs against the rear wall in the Miami Fish and Wildlife office. The Bat Cave was just a storage closet again. He switched on his portable radio. Actually, it was not his radio; he had borrowed it from Jennifer, but they both knew she was never going to get the thing back, not during baseball season. The Marlins had taken the World Series in 1997, the same year Van Nostrand was convicted. It was a banner year all the way around, but the following year the team's owner cried poverty and sold off all of his best ballplayers. The Marlins lost 108 games that season, dropping from king of the world to the bottom of the National League.

Bepler hoped the same would not be true of Van Nostrand. In fact, he had bet on it. He had supported giving Van Nostrand his license back early. Van Nostrand had made mistakes, and maybe he should have received a harsher punishment, but he got what the system gave him. That was the deal. The way Bepler saw it, if he treated Van Nostrand like an animal, then he was lost, too. And so he trusted Van Nostrand. Not blindly, of course, but enough to get him back on his feet. Trusting any convicted reptile smuggler not to repeat his crime was spitting in the eye of history. The best field guide in the world for identifying a top reptile smuggler was the criminal records database of the U.S. federal court system. Those who got caught usually repeated.

Van Nostrand had helped Bepler make a number of cases, and you don't work like that, with a man against himself, without coming to see a bit inside his heart. Van Nostrand would take advantage of you if you let him, but he was not the same person he had been before he'd entered prison, and that was something. That was something important as far as endangered species were concerned.

Van Nostrand had been a witness for the government in some prosecutions. These were "historical" cases, in which you found out about smuggling that had taken place in the past and put together evidence to prove it. Before Strictly Reptiles, the only cases being made on reptile smugglers were historical; the government just did not have the evidence to make a case against current criminal activity. Catching Van Nostrand gave them a lot of history. And knowing that Van Nostrand was willing to testify had led at least one defendant simply to give up.

Still, it was probably Van Nostrand's fault that they'd lost one of their slam-dunk cases. During the trial of Dwayne Cunningham, the cruise-ship comedian, it came out that Van Nostrand had referred to Cunningham once as a nigger. That terrible mouth of his. It did no good to argue to the jury that Van Nostrand wrote "Heil Hitler!" on shipments to his friend in Germany, that he drew swastikas on crates to a Jewish customer in New York, that he scrawled on crates to Italy, "Luca Brasi sleeps with the fishes." It would do no good to tell a jury that he was obnoxious and loud for reasons not even his mother understood.

The government convicted Cunningham and his divemaster smuggling partner in a second trial for their roles in smuggling reptiles out of Madagascar. In that trial, prosecutors had Mike's father testify.

After the Strictly Reptiles case, the Justice Department sent Bepler a letter. "You were nominated by the Wildlife and Marine Resources Section to receive a Special Commendation . . . for being primarily responsible for the three year investigation leading up to the indictment and conviction on multiple felony wildlife smuggling charges of Strictly Reptiles, Inc., the nation's largest reptile importing business."

The best part of the letter was the last line: "While we hope you plan to attend, we will, unfortunately, be unable to fund travel and associated costs for the event." That was the story of wildlife protection in America. He got a plaque in the mail a month later and put it with the others, in his bottom desk drawer.

He did accept an award in person once. It was for the Lucio Coronel case, the guy who'd said he was smuggling several hundred reptiles in his suitcase as a gift for the Bronx Zoo. The Beplers went as a family, and when Chip's name was called, he took their son, Robbie, up on stage with him, carrying the boy on his shoulders. Robin was proud of him for doing that. It seemed to Chip that taking your child along with you was the whole point.

Beware of what you wish for. Bepler had gotten it all with Strictly Repiles, and now he, too, was bored. He stood up from his chair and began walking in circles, tapping his finger against his thigh to think it through. Busting Van Nostrand and the South Florida reptile mafia, as some referred to it, was the tip of the iceberg as far as reptile crime went. Anson Wong was in prison, sentenced to seventy-one months, but Wong would be out soon. While he served his time, his wife ran his reptile business. Shipments were still coming in from Sungai Rusa Wildlife and CBS Wildlife, which were the same thing. The Malaysian government had not taken a single step to curb the world's most blatant wildlife smuggler.

Bepler had an idea. There were plenty of other targets out there, and he had a hell of a lot of knowledge now about who they were and how they operated. It did not have to be overseas, even. There were teams poaching rare species out West, in Arizona and down into Mexico.

Things had changed for him since Van Nostrand had gone to prison. Everybody he went after lay down and gave up. Nobody fought back. Van Nostrand? You pushed him in the smallest way and you knew he was coming back at you, on the attack with his lawyers. It was fun. That was the thing: it used to be fun.

He had become a bit of an addict himself, to the rush of the illicit deal, to the chase and the fight. In the progression from bigger to meaner to rarer to hot, Bepler was stuck on hot.

He picked up the telephone and called his college pal and best friend, Special Agent Dan Burleson. It was Burleson who'd gotten them work on the tuna boats out in California. That experience had taught them some valuable lessons: use one species to track another; throw a very large net and close it up slowly; break the rules and jump in to push out anything that might die; and, most of all, get out before commercialization of wildlife hardens you so much that you accept it.

It was Burleson who'd suggested that they take those first jobs as wildlife inspectors with Fish and Wildlife; Burleson who'd suggested that they put in to be special agents. He and Burleson had roomed together at FLETC, had gotten in a little trouble one time over a keg in a church van. Chip had been Burleson's best man, and if he and Robin had not secretly gone off to Switzerland to get married, it was a sure thing Burleson would have been his. His entire professional life, Dan Burleson had been there for him.

Now he had an idea for his lifelong friend. When Burleson answered the telephone, Bepler put it to him: What if we joined Special Operations?

Special Operations was the Fish and Wildlife Service's elite undercover squad. It was tiny, just five special agents, but what they did were big, long-term undercover investigations focused on the wildlife resources deemed most at risk from illegal commercial exploitation. Special Operations was a strike team.

George Morrison's PacRim takedown of Anson Wong had been an Ops investigation, part of Operation Chameleon. Jennifer English's success nabbing bird smugglers had folded into Operation Renegade, an Ops investigation that not only took down bird smugglers around the world but also resulted in a new federal law, the Wild Bird Conservation Act of 1992, which virtually shut down trade in wild-caught exotic bird species. If they worked for Ops, Bepler said, they could put together some amazing cases.

Burleson was settled out in Missouri. He was making good cases, deer poachers and the like. He had a good life, a family.

Bepler had thought of that already. Headquarters had said they would let him stay in Miami, so maybe Burleson could keep his home base, too. Bepler would be the brains of the operation and Burleson would do the undercover work. Burleson liked the idea of working with Chip again. Their boys were about the same age, so even moving down to Miami was a possibility. He said he would talk it over with his wife.

Bepler traveled to West Virginia for his routine in-service training. For special agents, the requirement was forty hours of in-service each year. Some years, training was held at an old CIA facility in Arizona; other years, when funds were low, each region put on its own training. This year, in-service was being held at the National Conservation Training Center, a brand-new university for conservation professionals operated by the U.S. Fish and Wildlife Service. NCTC hosted experts from around the world, and was also the repository for the service's history. What Bepler wanted to do next with his life was out in front of the history stored underground at NCTC. He wanted to be a part of history they had not made yet.

By coincidence, the most revered Ops agent in the service's history, Rick Leach, had recently retired and was receiving an award at this in-service. Leach was a twenty-eight-year veteran who had pioneered the service's long-term undercover technique. The entire Ops team would likely be on campus.

Even before Monday classes started, reptiles were the talk of the conference. On Saturday, actor Sharon Stone had surprised her husband with a behind-the-scenes tour of the Los Angeles Zoo's new Komodo dragon facility. Phil Bronstein had always wanted to see a Komodo dragon in person; the private tour was Stone's gift to him for Father's Day. "Would you like to go in the cage?" the zookeeper had asked him. Bronstein said he would, and following the keeper, he crawled through the dragon's narrow feed door into the enclosure, while Stone waited outside with a camera.

The dragon flicked its long tongue at Bronstein's white sneakers. He probably thinks they're food, the keeper said, explaining that the male was fed a diet of white rats. At the keeper's suggestion, Bronstein removed his shoes and then his socks, and so he was standing barefoot in the enclosure when the dragon attacked him. It started with his foot. Until recently, tourists to the Indonesian island of Komodo could pay twenty dollars to have a goat with its throat slit tossed to adult dragons and whiplashed to death. In the wild, Komodo dragons bowl, knock, or pull prey off its feet, thrash it, and then eat it. Their saliva is notoriously bacteria-loaded and, more recently, has been shown to contain venom. Bronstein stepped his heel down on the lizard's head and pried its jaws open but not before the animal had sliced through the tendons of his foot, nearly severing his big toe. Screaming and splashing blood, he scrambled feet-first back through the feed door, leaving a panicked zookeeper trapped in his own exhibit.

Team members of Special Operations couldn't believe it. Three years ago that same male Komodo dragon had emerged as a baby from James Burroughs's suitcase, emaciated and dehydrated, smuggled into the United States from Anson Wong. It was the smaller of the two dragons "suitcased" to Special Agent Morrison. When the dragon first arrived, it had slept nights inside a used paper towel roll. Now, according to news reports, it was ten-feet long and weighed over one hundred pounds.

It had always been nippy.

During one of the breaks in training sessions, Bepler asked to speak privately with Special Agent Sam Jojola, a member of Special Operations.

Jojola had been part of Operation Chameleon and was currently working Operation Botany, an investigation into the smuggling of primitive plants called cycads. His undercover name was Nelson DeLuca. As Nelson DeLuca, he was a real estate magnate who had a special passion for rare cycads. When it came to reptiles, a very different Nelson DeLuca owned Silverstate Exotics, which dealt in rare reptiles and birds. Over the years, Nelson DeLuca had sent a bunch of men to prison, and Sam Jojola had had a lot of fun doing it.

They met in Jojola's room. Bepler wanted to know more about Special Operations and whether he might fit in.

Jojola had signed up for the military when he was eighteen and joined the Army Rangers out of Fort Benning. He had served under Colonel Robert L. Howard (then captain), nominated three times for the Congressional Medal of Honor, and among the most decorated soldiers in American history. Colonel Howard had made a strong impression on Jojola, imprinting him with a measuring stick for what it took to be a leader: loyalty to those who serve below you, not above; passion; willingness to work in the trenches; and vision. Jojola had been honored to serve under Howard. To his amazement, he'd found the same qualities in Rick Leach.

During this in-service training, the National Fish and Wildlife Foundation was giving Leach the Guy Bradley Award, named for the South Florida investigator who became the first federal wildlife law enforcement officer killed in the line of duty. The Guy Bradley Award is given to "extraordinary individuals" in wildlife law enforcement, and is considered the highest award a conservation officer can receive. Leach, however, had refused to come to the in-service session to accept it. It was for his men, he said. Because Leach would not be there, Jojola intended to make a speech during the award ceremony to let the next generation of agents know who it was they were missing. To Jojola, Leach was a mastermind strategist and a leader in the Colonel Howard mold. Jojola's mind was heavy with fear that Leach's retirement might signal the end of an era for Special Operations and, given limited funding, maybe even worse than that. He did not care to diminish Special Operations by taking on men who were not up to Leach's caliber.

Jojola had heard of Bepler. They had a mutual friend named Ken McCloud; he'd gone to FLETC training with Bepler and was currently working undercover with Jojola. McCloud was the most knowledgeable reptile man in the Fish and Wildlife Service. He could have been a herpetologist, but he had a talent, too, for managing complex operations and had made an art out of impersonating bad guys. At the moment, McCloud was back in California preparing a takedown. From what Jojola had heard from McCloud, Bepler had vision, a willingness to look at all of the wildlife crime going on in the United States and ask, What is the engine, and how do I stop it?

Bepler was asking Jojola a lot of preliminary questions, but Jojola could see in his eyes that spark that appears when a person has already made up his mind. Bepler wanted in. To Jojola, Bepler was perfect for Special Operations. Even better, Ops was planning a covert operation based in two port cities, one of which was Miami. Nobody was pleased with the sentences they were getting out of Miami. Bepler, too, would have liked more. Now he might have a second chance at it. It would be U.S. Fish and Wildlife's first long-term undercover operation in Miami, and when it was over, Bepler and his family could decide whether the Ops life was for them. If it was not his thing, he could return to his old job in the Miami office. "You should apply," Jojola told Bepler.

It was a day in the fall, just three months after the in-service training, that he got the headache. A lightning flash, out of the blue. He was playing catch with his son, he would later say, and his arm would not throw right. His speech was off. He thought maybe he was having a stroke. He was not.

He never got sick. Never. As a boy Bepler was so rarely ill that the one time he did get sick his mother, who was a nurse, panicked. But soon enough Dr. Bepler and his wife heard a *thump, swish, thump, thump, thump, swish* that told them Chip was out front shooting baskets into the night.

The diagnosis was glioblastoma multiforme (GBM), the most aggressive form of brain tumor. Bepler was forty-five years old. His doctor told him he had one to two years to live.

He refused to die. "I am not going to live the end of my life thinking about dying," he told Robin. "I am going to live." It was late September 2001. The country lay blanketed in grief. The Beplers went skiing that winter in Colorado. Chip went fishing with his father and his brothers.

Burleson called as soon as he heard. "Hey, pal, what's going on?"

"Oh, I went to the doctor," Bepler said.

"What did he say?"

"I got the big salami."

"What's that?" Burleson asked, wanting more.

"I got the big salami," Bepler said.

Dan Burleson came down with his son Tom and they took a camping trip together in the Keys, just the two fathers and their boys. They snorkeled and fished, and let their sons cuss a little.

Chip Bepler lived for twenty-five months. It was strange. GBM occurs in just three out of 100,000 people, and yet another man who as a boy had fished with Chip over near the power plant had also died recently of GBM. It said nothing really, but it left Chip's father wondering, agonizing, over a son who had loved to fish.

They came from all over the United States—federal prosecutors, U.S. Fish and Wildlife Service agents, Department of Interior officials, Florida Fish and Game officers. The state of Florida provided its honor guard, who performed what they called the death watch: a silent march, in dress uniform and white gloves, around the perimeter of the chapel in honor of the fallen.

Van Nostrand walked in late. He wore the same suit he had worn at his sentencing six years earlier. He heard the whispers. *That's Mike Van Nostrand from Strictly Reptiles. That's Mike Van Nostrand.*

Here was the entire machine at work to stop him, the skin pulled back from a dissected frog. He did not recognize many of these people, but there was no doubt most of them had seen him on the recent BBC-MSNBC joint investigative report *Animal Smugglers*. On the program, he and Tom Crutchfield were portrayed as the two American villains, while Anson Wong was the supply world's kingpin. Van Nostrand only had one decent line in the program. It came in answer to BBC reporter Tom Mangold's question about why he smuggled. "It was purely for profit," he said. It became his nickname with Tommy Crutchfield. "Mr. Purely for Profit," Crutchfield called him now. "Mr. Conservation Through Commercialization," Van Nostrand called Crutchfield.

Some of the federal officials walked up to Van Nostrand, introduced themselves, and shook his hand. He did not know why—maybe because of the help he had given Chip after his arrest, or maybe because they thought of him as a trophy and wanted to touch him. He felt like Don Corleone.

He heard a voice he recognized.

"What is he doing here?" Jennifer English demanded.

Van Nostrand saw John West, the Florida Fish and Game officer who had introduced him to Bepler twelve years earlier. It was Captain John West now. "John," he said, "let me sit with you." He quickly took a seat beside West.

One by one Bepler's loved ones and colleagues got up to speak. They told stories about their friend, their brother, his life. Tom Watts-Fitzgerald, prosecutor on the Strictly Reptiles case, recalled the first time he'd met Chip. Bepler had knocked on his door and introduced himself, telling the naive prosecutor he had a great lizard-smuggling case to discuss over lunch. He'd brought the evidence with him, he said, holding up cloth bags. On their way out the door Bepler paused. "We should let them stretch their legs a little," he told Watts-Fitzgerald. The lizards were tegus, a large South American species much like a monitor. Watts-Fitzgerald shrugged his okay; Bepler dumped the lizards out of the bag and shut the prosecutor's door.

When they returned there were lizards running everywhere. They had torn the prosecutor's desk apart. Bepler was in tears. It was a laugh you could not forget, Watts-Fitzgerald said, and everyone in the room nodded to themselves. They would not forget his laugh, they were sure of that.

Captain John West nudged Van Nostrand. "Say something, Mike."

Van Nostrand looked at West. "Are you crazy?"

"You're the one person in this room that lets people know their job makes a difference," West said. "Go ahead."

Van Nostrand raised his hand. Then he stood up and walked to the front of the room. "My name is Mike Van Nostrand," he said. "And I may be one of the most unique individuals in this room, because I was one of Chip's cases..."

He told the room what a good father he knew Chip was, what a tenacious investigator, and what a great loss he would be to the U.S. Fish and Wildlife Service. Chip had hurt him, hurt his business, he said. "If Bepler was on you, you were done," he had come to say many times. And Mike believed something else, too: if Chip hadn't come down from New York, he never would have stopped smuggling. Not ever.

Van Nostrand's lawyer, Patrick O'Brien, had likewise come to think of Bepler as a wonder, an investigator who used the full force of the law to pursue his target, the kind of investigator O'Brien had wished for when he was in law enforcement. Bepler just kept coming at you.

Van Nostrand told the room that Chip Bepler had changed his life, made him realize the error of his ways. "I'm gonna miss him," he said.

Afterward, he heard a deep voice calling out among the mourners. "Where is he?" the voice asked. He heard it again: "Where is he?"

It was Dr. Bepler. Chip never thought of you the same as the others, he told Van Nostrand. He shook Van Nostrand's hand.

The Chameleon

Van Nostrand asked his supplier in Russia about chameleons. The ones he was interested in came from Madagascar. The Russian had them, she said, and gave him her price. He did the math and decided that he could make a thousand dollars apiece on the lizards. He asked how many she had available.

Four hundred, she said. There was just one catch: they had no papers. They were illegal.

That was $400,000 pure profit!

He walked outside and got into his truck. He and Michelle had had another baby, a boy, bringing their family to three boys and one girl. He had not named any of his sons Michael. Mike was a bad kid's name. Name your kid Mike and you were locking him into his future. He said the word to himself sometimes: *Mike*.

He had another line he said to himself at times like this: *I'm the bad guy*. It was what Al

Pacino's character yelled in the movie *Scarface,* in the restaurant with all those nice people staring up from their filet mignons. He knew the scene by heart.

Him, Hank, Tommy, Anson—they were the bad guys. Walk into any pet store in America and the cute little lizard you see there on the sand is an Australian bearded dragon. Australia doesn't let anything out. How the fuck do people think the original breeders on those lizards got here? Where do people think the zoos got a lot of their original stock? Frilled dragons were a hundred and fifty bucks apiece in pet stores now because of him. You could buy them on the Internet—legitimate, captive-bred frilled dragons, because of him.

Everybody bent the rules. Insider trading? Martha Stewart played with a little inside information, but do you think if it was anybody besides Martha Stewart anybody would give a shit about what she did? People do that every single day, make small compromises. Did she do wrong? Absolutely. Did she deserve what she got? No.

It was because of who he was—*Strictly Reptiles . . . Mike Van Nostrand*—that the government came after him. If we ate turtles the way we eat lobster in this country, they would be treating him differently. Lobsters are an ugly thing because we eat them. He had a whole list of beefs on how the system fed on its own self-interest.

He lived in a gated community called Imagination Farms. As he approached its entrance, he waved down to the guard from the window of his truck. The guard opened the gate, and he drove over a little brick bridge and along a manicured route to his home.

He had recently installed a train horn in his truck, a real train horn. That was illegal, too, but it was funny as hell to hit the button and watch a neighborhood kid fall off his skateboard onto somebody's lawn. It was even funnier to drive over to Weston, where all the snobs ate at those sidewalk restaurants, and let loose on the horn. *Bad guy coming through!*

What did he care? People had tried to outlaw his truck from the community. His next-door neighbor believed he was a drug dealer. "You can't make that kind of money selling reptiles," the guy had said to him once.

That night he tried to sleep, but he couldn't. The next night it was the same thing. Four hundred thousand dollars.

His father had ideas for making money. A Louisiana congressman was proposing to do away with the four-inch-turtle rule to enable turtle farmers to sell baby turtles again in the United States. The idea captivated Ray, whose favorite reptile was the baby turtle. "Turtles are green, the color of money," he'd say. "They're good luck in most countries, and the Chinese eat them."

Ray had some other ideas, too, like letting endangered wood turtles go on some land he owned and then getting the Nature Conservancy to buy it.

"We need to clean this place up," Mike yelled at him one afternoon.

"Why don't we get that blind girl in here that likes to give blow jobs," Ray suggested.

Mike walked out of the building. "Why can't I have a normal father?" he said, shaking his head. He wanted a father who came to his boys' Little League games, the way his mother did.

His conversation with the Russian exporter had been via e-mail. She'd written in her e-mail that the chameleons were wild-caught but she could get them captive-bred paperwork. *She'd written it down.* If she had said nothing about the paperwork, he would have done the deal. That he knew for certain.

He stared at his computer screen. He could feel his blood pressure climbing, just like it used to do, back when life was fun.

He read her e-mail again.

All he had to do was type out a single word. It was a word so small almost nobody would notice it. All he had to do was type the word *yes.* What were the odds that Fish and Wildlife was behind her offer—a Madagascar chameleon shipped out of Russia?

He did know the answer to one question: if Chip were around, he would not be losing sleep over the deal because he would *know* it was a setup.

Now there was only a chance that it was.

He decided to work it both ways. He let the Russian think he was interested in her smuggling proposal, and then he called the Miami office and told U.S. Fish and Wildlife about it.

It was a brilliant strategy. If the e-mail *was* part of a sting operation, then telling the government about her offer turned the sting attempt into an asset: he was not a smuggler, and calling them on a great deal proved it, so they should stop looking at him.

If the e-mail was not part of a sting operation, then he was doing U.S. Fish and Wildlife a favor. They could go after the Russian, he could earn himself a deposit in the favor bank, *and* he could keep himself in the loop business-wise. There was a chance he might make some money on the transaction yet.

The Miami office turned his offer down. He was not

surprised. To make their case, the government would have to spend a lot of money, allow a lot of smuggling, and then have to lure the Russian into the United States. Odds were that even if they turned it into a long-term undercover operation, they would still never get an arrest.

He sat down at his computer and typed his response to the Russian. If Chip were alive, Mike was pretty sure, he would have taken the case. Not to get the arrest, but just to know.

Inside the door of the Miami Division of Law Enforcement, U.S. Fish and Wildlife Service, hanging just above the light switch, is a photograph of Special Agent Charles Robert Bepler Jr. In it, he wears a baseball cap and has grown a light beard. Bepler is smiling; his arm is around his young son, a roller-hockey player. His is the first face agents see when they turn on the lights in the morning, and the last before they go home.

Author's Note

In our first interview, Mike Van Nostrand agreed to talk to me about anything except reptile smuggling. Between the BBC and local newspapers, he had had enough negative publicity, he said. To convince him that I might be different, I dredged up a vague memory of a pet store my mother used to take me to on my birthday: "When I was in high school there was a place in Philadelphia called Martin's—" I began. Van Nostrand did not let me finish. "Martin's Aquarium," he said, and looked at me a little strangely.

We continued working through the list of questions he had asked me to fax him in advance of our meeting, but off and on I could see that something was bothering him. When his father entered the office, Van Nostrand introduced me by saying, "He used to go to Martin's Aquarium." Ray's eyes sparkled the way a person's do when they recall a favorite adventure. Given what I knew of Ray's life, I figured it would have to be some story.

Martin's Aquarium, just north of Philadelphia, was a Willy Wonka factory of tropical fish, parrots, and an entire section of wild reptiles from all over the world. It bubbled and wheezed with pet-shop smells and sounds, cracks and screeches, and anxious people packed shoulder to shoulder. Often on weekends there was a line to get in the door, and certainly there was a line to get out, with animals. One of the owners, Joel Zisholtz, sat in a raised booth in the middle of the store, calling out numbers for pickup, New York delicatessen–style.

Two hours away, in southern New Jersey, we heard about Martin's Aquarium. In my neighborhood we traded reptiles and amphibians the way other kids trade baseball cards. A pickerel frog got you a box turtle; two box turtles got you a "blue belly" fence swift. No amount of trading could get you a snake. If you had a snake, you did not trade it, ever. In second grade, I brought a kingsnake to school for show-and-tell. My father, the town mortician, drove me to school in his Cadillac, something he never did. Kids gathered, naturally; teachers from other grades poked their heads into the classroom; older boys stopped me in the hallway; the principal called me to his office so he could look inside my pillowcase. I don't think I ever recovered from the celebrity I achieved simply for holding what other people were afraid of, what they had been taught was wrong.

The night before my mother was going to take me to Martin's Aquarium I could not sleep. The first time I walked in I lost my balance; I was dizzy. It's vertigo, my mother said. I got it every time I went into the store.

Like Ray Van Nostrand, I became the boy in town the police told you to call if you found a snake in your bushes. Also like Ray, I gave talks about snakes to local schools. On weekends, I could be found picking through garbage on the edge of the local pond, or hiking through the woods, lifting up logs and rocks. I spent many afternoons as a boy lying on my bed with the same books Hank Molt and Ray Van Nostrand read. On trips to the Philadelphia Zoo, I stayed as long as possible in the reptile house they'd visited so often.

Unlike Ray, I outgrew reptiles. The week I left home for college I gave away Socrates, a twelve-foot, rabbit-eating Burmese python I had raised from the size of a candy cane. My freshman year I won a writing award for a story I wrote about Socrates called "The Big Gulp." "The Big Gulp" helped me get into law school in 1988—the same year Ray was going to prison and Mike was opening Strictly Reptiles. Like a good Washington, D.C., lawyer, I soon built myself a nice little Habitrail and scurried to work dressed like I was headed to a funeral.

I had grown up riding casket carts as pirate ships, seeing babysitters and schoolteachers and other people from town on a table in our back room. In college, I had embalmed a neighbor I'd gone to grade school with. But my father's premature death shook loose the boy I had once been and made me ask myself what I cared about. It was not law; it was writing. And once I opened that door, I knew I wanted to write something about reptiles. I knew that some of the top reptile dealers had criminal records. I decided to look into it.

I met Mike Van Nostrand in the summer of 2004. It turned out, of course, that the reason he looked at me strangely during our interview was in part because the man who ran the reptiles department at Martin's Aquarium, Bob Udell, had gotten Mike started in the reptile business and had worked with his father in the narcotics business. Udell had also been a codefendant with Hank Molt in the trial that altered the Lacey Act, inspiring the president to call for a wildlife crimes section at the Justice Department.

Martin's Aquarium had other links to people in Mike's life and in my research. Martin's Aquarium was where Dwayne Cunningham shopped for snakes as a boy. It was blocks from the house where Hank Molt grew up. It was Ray's major pet-store customer when he was starting out in New York, and Ray continued to supply Martin's Aquarium from Pet Farm, and from Mario Tabraue's Zoological Imports.

I discovered those coincidences over time, and each time I heard a reference to Martin's Aquarium, it seemed to me to be a reminder that there was magic to be found, if I didn't try so hard.

Over the next three and a half years Van Nostrand broke his promise not to talk to me about his smuggling. Eventually, I rented an apartment and moved to Florida for several months. I wasn't there long before Ray gave me a job in the snake room, cleaning cages, feeding snakes, watering tarantulas, and taking inventory. As payment, Mike and I had lunches together and he answered my questions about the reptile world, and his smuggling.

At Mike's direction, his lawyer, Patrick O'Brien, turned over to me his unsanitized legal files, spanning the six years from Medina's arrest through Mike's imprisonment. They were brought out of storage, and I packed six banker's boxes into my pickup truck. A man tells his lawyer many things over the years, so this was an amazing gift. It was not my only good fortune. The U.S. Fish and Wildlife Service provided thousands of pages of telephone transcripts and investigative reports, in addition to allowing me access to agents across the country. Team Aura leader Henry Ligtenberg provided assistance from the Netherlands, as did Dr. Willie Smits in Indonesia. Chip Bepler's personal notes became available to me. *America's Most Wanted* shared with me their coverage of the Medina arrest. The U.S. Attorney's Office in Miami made its prosecutors available throughout South Florida. I met in person with every major character in this book, including Mario Tabraue, Hank Molt, Tommy Crutchfield, Andre Van Meer in Indonesia, and Anson Wong in Penang. Nothing was made up. I took no literary license.

What Robin Bepler and the rest of Chip's family gave me, a stranger, in talking to me about a man they had only recently lost is beyond my ability to know or express. It is worth saying publicly what headquarters wrote to me when I told them about this project: "He was one of our best."

In researching this book, I found myself drawn to the subject of wonder. I spent a good deal of time trying to distill what it was in my childhood that I had not been able to find in adulthood prior to meeting the Van Nostrands. I came upon references to the medieval *Liber Monstrorum*, the "Book of Monsters." Written during the period of man's own intellectual childhood, the Book of Monsters was an attempt to catalog the world's sources of wonder, its "secret arrangements," presenting them in order from the most accepted to the most horrible, bolstering as the list unfolded what it meant to be human. The anonymous author began the book to his lord by reminding him that he had asked his writer to search out: "the three types of things that provoke greatest terror in the human race, monstrous human births, the horrible and innumerable types of wild beasts, and the most terrible kinds of dragons, serpents, and vipers."

In this story I expected to go to the lip of the world and find abhorrent creatures. I found some so repugnant I had to worry about their effect on me. But I also found humanity: Mike Van Nostrand sacrificed an accounting career for his family; Chip Bepler insisted that suspects be treated as human beings. I found love and passion more intense in the Van Nostrand family than that which I had experienced in my own family or observed in families I'd seen as a lawyer in Washington, D.C.

Martin's Aquarium.

We are all connected, even by reptiles, and there is beauty in that, too.

Acknowledgments

This book would not exist without my agent, International Creative Management's Jennifer Joel, who was willing to get her hands dirty taking on a reptile story. Early on Jenn asked me to explain my personal connection to reptiles, a history I had forgotten, and subsequently she pushed to bring out the heart of others in this story. You know you are a good fit when you call up about your reptile book and your agent tells you she is off to the Galápagos Islands.

To my initial proposal, Jonathan Karp, my editor and publisher at Twelve, replied, "Bull's-eye!" Jon then showed me where the target was, emphasizing that beauty is in simplicity, and that nonfiction both derives its entertainment power and deserves its place when every fact can be trusted. Nate Gray at Twelve managed this book along the way, and Cary Goldstein of Twelve ensured that somebody heard about it. If I could marry copyeditor Bonnie Thompson I would, but I have never spoken with her. She listened to this story with a stethoscope, and together with the above team gave it life.

Acknowledgments

I owe a special debt of gratitude to Mike Van Nostrand, who opened his doors to me for three and a half years, as did his family. Likewise, I am indebted to the Bepler family, especially to Chip's father for taking me through his son's life, and to Chip's wife, Robin, for sharing stories of her husband. Robin Bepler has returned to the U.S. Fish and Wildlife Service and is a wildlife inspector at the Port of Miami. Dr. Bepler passed away before this book was finished; meeting him was one of the great joys of this project.

The Law Enforcement Division of the U.S. Fish and Wildlife Service has to be the most underappreciated, worst-funded body in our federal government, and yet we put in its care our country's wildlife (and the world's). As this book goes to print the Special Operations Branch is in jeopardy. I owe a great deal to the following: Dan Burleson, Sandra Cleva, Marion Dean, Vance Eaddy, Jennifer English, Terry English, Sam Jojola, Lennie Jones, Saverio "Sam" LiBrandi, Ernest Mayer, Ken and Rose McCloud, Eddie McKissick, and George Morrison (the name "Karl Hart" was fabricated for security reasons).

Magistrate Judge Chris McAliley. Judge McAliley's story was one of several that stands on its own for leadership. Likewise, the story of U.S. Customs agent Joseph O'Kane and former Assistant U.S. Attorney Tom Mellon, whose work was the opposite of Pyrrhic—the Molt case they fought brought about legal and structural changes at the foundation of environmental law enforcement today.

Current and former Assistant U.S. Attorneys and Justice Department officials Robert S. Anderson, Antonia Barnes, Kenneth Berlin, Lauren Jorgensen, James W. Moorman, Michael Nerney, Tom Watts-Fitzgerald, and John T. Webb were all very helpful.

Ralph Davis, the rock star of designer breeding, took

me in, as did Bob Applegate, Brian Barczyk, Mark and Kim Bell, Bob Clark, Pete Kahl, Bill and Kathy Love, and Kevin McCurley; Dave and Tracy Barker at V.P.I. have produced a book on ball pythons that should be on the coffee table of anyone who cares about art.

Kamuran Tepedlen put up with me for many miles in Indonesia. Brian Potter literally walked me through the who's who of the reptile world, and Wayne Hill of the National Reptile Breeders' Expo gave me the pass to do it. Jeanne Brodsky of Strictly Reptiles nearly killed me when we first met; later she let me shoot her .38, and even better has become a friend. Tom Crutchfield was particularly generous with his time. Dwayne Cunningham was terrific, though his raccoon did steal the meat off my cheeseburger. Joel Zisholtz, an owner of Martin's Aquarium, and I returned to Martin's together. It is a mattress store today. What used to be the reptiles department is much smaller than I'd remembered, but Joel said that is because I am much bigger.

Dr. Joseph B. Slowinski died during a herpetological expedition in Myanmar in September 2001. For a time, this book might have been Joe's story and to that end I owe a great deal of thanks to his friends and colleagues, including Dr. Jeff Boundy, Dr. Brian Crother, Dr. Bryan Grieg Fry, Armin Meier, Mark O'Shea, Dr. Mary White, Dr. Wolfgang Wuster, and Dr. George Zug.

Art Bass and Jack Lowris both passed away during the writing of this book. They do not appear in the narrative but it was great fun to have spent time with them; they were last of a breed of animal adventurers.

National Geographic was very supportive in giving me time to complete this project. I thank, of course, all those others named in this book, and those nameless who were behind it.

About the Author

Bryan Christy, a former lawyer and a Fulbright scholar, has freelanced for *Playboy* and *National Geographic.* While researching this book he was bitten between the eyes by a blood python, chased by a mother alligator, sprayed by a bird-eating tarantula, and ejaculated on by a Bengal tiger. He is a member of the Society for the Study of Amphibians and Reptiles. He can be reached at BryanChristy.com.

ABOUT TWELVE

TWELVE was established in August 2005 with the objective of publishing no more than one book per month. We strive to publish the singular book, by authors who have a unique perspective and compelling authority. Works that explain our culture; that illuminate, inspire, provoke, and entertain. We seek to establish communities of conversation surrounding our books. Talented authors deserve attention not only from publishers, but from readers as well. To sell the book is only the beginning of our mission. To build avid audiences of readers who are enriched by these works—that is our ultimate purpose.

For more information about forthcoming TWELVE books, you can visit us at www.twelvebooks.com.